VICTIM TO VICTOR

A Year in the Life of a University President

Harold H. Haak

American Association of State Colleges and Universities

© 1987 by American Association of State Colleges and Universities
Washington, D.C.

The names of characters and institutions in this book are entirely fictitious, and any resemblance to real persons or places is unintentional.

Library of Congress Cataloging-in-Publication Data

Haak, Harold H.
   Victim to victor.

   Sequel to: Parable of a president. 1982.
   1. College presidents—United States. 2. Universities and colleges—United States—Administration. I. Title.
LB2341.H24   1988   378'.111   88-4
ISBN   0-88044-092-9

Contents

Preface **v**

Chapter 1 **1**

Chapter 2 **4**

Chapter 3 **15**

Chapter 4 **20**

Chapter 5 **27**

Chapter 6 **31**

Chapter 7 **37**

Chapter 8 **45**

Chapter 9 **54**

Chapter 10 **64**

Chapter 11 **72**

About the Author **77**

Preface

In many ways this book is a sequel to *Parable of a President,* also published by the American Association of State Colleges and Universities. Again, Hubert Jones is the principal character, Linden State University the setting, and one school year in the life of President Jones the format.

In *Parable of a President* my purpose was to illustrate "up-tight management" and its mix of conflict-oriented organizational models with those that deny or deemphasize conflict. As I noted in the Afterword to *Parable,* "The focus is not on Jones per se, but instead on his situation. Basic to the argument of the narrative is the thesis that the situation leads inexorably to 'up-tight management.'"

In this new book we find an older Hubert Jones who himself has grown "up-tight." In one of those flashes of middle-aged courage we dream about but rarely experience, Jones resolves he no longer will permit himself to be victimized. He will strike back! He will assert himself, accomplish things at Linden State he had always wanted to do, and then quit the presidency a winner in his own eyes.

Especially in view of Jones's penchant to end up in trouble, let me issue the usual and important denials: I am not Hubert Jones but, after two narratives, I am afraid he's beginning to influence my behavior. The other characters are fictitious, too, although I hope they are stereotypical enough to remind the reader of many people he or she has met before. Finally, Linden State certainly is not Fresno State; in particular, we take athletics much more seriously at Fresno!

In closing, my special thanks to my associates Harold L. Best and Marjorie Johnson for their assistance and encouragement; to Joanne L. Erickson, who provided editorial guidance and direction; and to my wife, Betty, without whose love and support I, too, would have been "up-tight" many times over.

1

Hubert Jones was frustrated. Or angry? Or did it make any difference, he wondered. At first he thought he was simply undergoing the normal decompression following the close of another academic year as president of Linden State University, but when he failed to bounce back in a week, he decided his world had somehow changed.

Understandably, at commencement time he was not in the best of moods. The close of the academic year found the faculty sniping at him for failing to provide academic leadership and blaming his administration for Linden State's drop in student enrollments. The students found him stuffy, and the fat, long-nosed president in the dull suit entangled in red tape in the cartoon appearing in the end-of-the-year spoof edition of the student newspaper irritated Hubert. The university staff members were vexed at the administration and had made much ado because a special dining area had been provided the faculty but no such privilege had been extended to them. Hubert also suspected that the outcry of "university elitism" filling the student council meetings and the student newspaper at the end of the year had started in the conference rooms of the student affairs division, where the counselors were especially enraged about being barred from the faculty dining area. To top it all off, the sports pages of the *Linden Times,* the self-proclaimed voice of the community, constantly harped that the university should go "big time" in athletics, and the faculty's budget committee was sniffing through university records to expose what members suspected to be a misallocation of instructional resources to the athletics program.

Normally, Hubert would have placed all these annoyances in proper perspective. He had been twenty years a university faculty member and academic administrator at three universities and each year had survived similar irritants. In fact, on this particular morning, his wife, Gladys, had tired of his morose mood during breakfast and had sharply reminded him that in his own faculty days he had caused more than one university president to have heartburn, especially when he had been chairman of the faculty senate and had campaigned to eliminate all special parking privileges for administrators.

But Hubert had lost his sense of equilibrium. He felt pushed too hard, for too long. Everything seemed to be getting out of hand. The students' behavior at commencement had been a good example. Perhaps he had gone too far in instructing the marshals to frisk students suspected of carrying champagne bottles under their robes, yet for most of the ceremony Hubert sensed improved deportment in the graduates' seating section. True, a few corks popped, and there was the usual assortment of garish headgear, paper airplanes, confetti, and whoops and hollers. Everyone, though, including Hubert, had a good time. Then there was the streaker—it looked like a streaker, although the lithe form covered in body paint moved so quickly and daringly that no one later was quite certain. Hubert was even secretly pleased that the green-and-yellow figure had disappeared unapprehended. The perpetrator had had the decency to paint himself in Linden State's school colors, and Hubert was in no mood to face another complicated student disciplinary hearing and renewed arguments about due process.

Hubert had been rather proud of how he had handled himself at the commencement ceremony. He thought he projected just the right amount of dignity and of empathy for the joy felt by those seniors who shortly would be counted among the cherished alumni of Linden State. He had become totally unglued, however, during recognition of the engineering students, when a model airplane buzzed and sputtered over the speaker's podium and then unloaded its cargo and crashed. There was the pop-pop-pop of firecrackers, a grass fire, and a pandemoniacal 15-minute interruption of commencement as the small but threatening blaze was put out. By the time order was restored, Hubert was completely discombobulated, but this was his seventh Linden State commencement and he was somehow able to struggle through the rest of his ceremonial lines. He knew he had rushed the recessional march, but he was anxious to get someplace where he could check his beloved orange Princeton doctoral robe to see if those really were oil spots from that flying instrument of technological terror.

Breakfast over, the morning paper read, and Gladys kissed good-bye, Hubert began the trek across campus from the president's home, an imposing on-campus edifice revealing no hint of its creaks and aging innards to passersby and the bane not only of his family but of his 11 predecessors, to his far more comfortable office. Jean, his wise secretary, sensed his mood early on, gave him a pleasant hello, and let him retreat to the quiet of his office to cope with his wounds from the year. Besides, this was her morning to leave early to have her hair done, and she was determined not to let the president's troubled emotional state ruin her day.

As soon as he was securely seated behind his seven-foot-wide, prison-constructed desk, Hubert felt presidential and tore into the stack of morning mail. In 15 minutes he was done. Returning phone calls took another 15 minutes. Because Linden State's summer schedule had already begun, Hubert suddenly found he had time—to think, to plan, and even to read the stack of articles and books on the handsome credenza behind his desk. But before such ponderous activity, Hubert realized he would have to get a better grip on himself. Perhaps, he decided, he should first attack a small problem, something soluble, and then go on to bigger things. He spent the next 20 minutes fantasizing how he could spring loose a convict gang to do the needed repairs on his house. Would a foundation be interested in providing grant money for an innovative prisoner release program? Eventually he gave up the effort as insoluble and probably ill-advised and turned his attention more productively to coping with his own mood.

For seven years he had given his all for Linden State, or at least that is how he saw it. Each school year had been an endurance contest of speeches, dinners, sports events, plays, art shows, and meetings—meetings with faculty and staff members, students, community groups, and the board of regents. He was called upon simultaneously to be "the boss"—responsible for everything—and the "spokesperson of the faculty"—effective director of very little. What had promised to be the capstone of his academic career—a college presidency—was taking on more and more signs of a struggle he was not going to win.

In one of those moments of certainty he seldom had any longer, Hubert Jones decided he was through being a victim. He was tired of adapting to and meeting the needs of others. He was going to assert himself, to accomplish some things at Linden State he had always wanted to do, and to leave the presidency a winner in his own eyes.

2

Gladys Jones was surprised that this time her husband seemed serious about controlling his weight and getting into shape. Over the past several years she had watched his paunch grow, had lectured and nagged him about his eating habits, and had tired of his excuses about the social pressures of a college presidency. When Hubert's diet and exercise regimen lasted more than a week, she sensed something had gotten his attention, and she knew it wasn't a delayed response to her previous pleas. In the meantime, she would share in Hubert's new-found enthusiasm for life; she decided she might even find an opportune moment to suggest that her mother join them in their spacious home, now that their children had left.

Physically, Hubert was starting to feel good for the first time in years. His daily morning regimen included half an hour on his stationary bike, followed by ten minutes on his rowing machine. From time to time he even biked across campus to his office; at other times, he walked briskly. Some eyebrows rose when he joined the staff wellness program, including the noon aerobics class, but he soon found acceptance within the group. Sweatsuits and jocks are great equalizers, he decided. Hubert squirmed somewhat when he overheard two instructors chuckling over the results of his body fat test, and wondered how far the news about his true obesity had traveled. The experience, however, strengthened his resolve to lie when taking the psychological profile required of all participants in the fitness program.

For some weeks Hubert had been dressing for the noon aerobics class in his office quarters when he decided he should either press for the installation of a shower in his private bathroom or seek out a locker in the men's locker room. There had been enough complaints when he had refurbished his office in the third year of his presidency, so he quickly dismissed the thought of requisitioning a private shower. Besides, the total cost would come to more than $10,000, which would have required a potentially embarrassing review of the minor construction request by the state office of contracts.

For a moment, while requesting a locker from the by-the-rules attendant, Hubert reconsidered. He was used to being recognized as president and treated appropriately, but the locker room attendant had no idea who he was and certainly was not going to issue a precious space in the faculty locker room until Jones provided proper identification. In turn, Hubert had long since lost his faculty—or was it *staff*—identification card and felt as helpless as a freshman at the end of a long line on the last day of registration. At first Hubert was amused, experiencing firsthand the intrinsically democratic nature of the world of athletics. Then he became irritated as he realized how importantly a head coach would be treated by the same attendant and how rigidly hierarchical the world of athletics really was. Fortunately, the athletics director happened by and immediately recognized Jones's predicament. Within moments Jones was outfitted with a complete set of gear; "large" sizes were hurriedly and skillfully exchanged for "extra large" without a hint of embarrassment; and Hubert was personally escorted to his locker by the athletics director. The only price he had to pay was listening to a 15-minute peroration about the need for more administrative support of Linden State's budding athletics program and the need for a new locker room and shower for the head coaches—and, of course, for the president.

"Hubert! Didn't expect to see you here." The voice belonged to John Carlson, an assistant dean of students for whom Hubert didn't care much. Carlson was overfamiliar and brash. He had been a star basketball player at Linden State some ten years earlier and president of the student body in his senior year. Like others of his kind Hubert had met through the years, Carlson simply stayed on after graduating and somehow survived. First he worked with the intramurals program, then became an activities coordinator, and finally an assistant dean of students with responsibility for student government, the fraternities and sororities, and an odd lot of special programs. Jones thought he was an arrogant pain in the behind and a possible contributor to endless student mischief. If Hubert had a list of campus undesirables, Carlson would rank near the top.

"Good seeing you again, Carlson," Hubert lied. "Working out regularly?"

"Well, I like to stay in shape. Try to run a couple of miles a day. Play some racquetball. Swim a few laps. You know."

Carlson's response confirmed Hubert's dislike of the younger man.

"Which exercise do you find the most beneficial?" Hubert asked, irritated with himself for prolonging the conversation.

"Racquetball," Carlson replied immediately. "It's a great sweat game and requires little time for a real workout. On top of that, it's easy to learn and can be real competitive. Want to give it a try? You've no doubt played some tennis and you'd catch on quick. Come on, I'll give you a lesson."

Some ten minutes and a visit to the equipment counter later, Jones found himself in the racquetball court with Carlson, who proved to be a patient instructor and a consummate politician, taking care to praise Hubert's awkward efforts, even when he missed the ball entirely with a roundhouse, tennis-style smash. Forty minutes later, Carlson, feigning tiredness, brought the session to a halt, much to Jones's relief. At the close of the session Hubert didn't like Carlson any better but had gained a clearer understanding of the man's success in moving up the student affairs career ladder. More important, Jones had had fun during those 40 minutes, and his eagerness in accepting regular Tuesday and Thursday games with Carlson surprised even himself.

In the third week of their matches, Hubert finally accomplished a major feat: he actually won a game. He was dismayed, though, when he discovered Carlson had been toying with him by playing left-handed. Playing right-handed, Carlson proceeded to whomp him—21 to 2—as if in retribution, thereby confirming Jones's original dislike of the man. As they played in the fourth week, Jones felt as if he were starting over against his right-handed opponent.

Over the summer Hubert occasionally played racquetball with an assortment of other opponents including the head football and basketball coaches. Gradually his conditioning program paid off: his weight dropped from 215 to 185, and he found he was able to give the coaches and others real competition, much to their surprise and, sometimes, chagrin. These court battles also gave him new insights into people he had previously seen only in well-choreographed roles.

ઠ   ઠ   ઠ

The head football coach, Don Whitman, had come to Linden State from a successful career as a community college coach in California just before Hubert had become president. Prior to his reign,

Linden State had wallowed around in a nonscholarship program and had been walloped regularly by the likes of New Mexico Highlands and the Colorado School of Mines. A 49-0 loss to Highlands was too much for the townspeople interested in the program; the old coach was dumped and sent on to a full-time teaching assignment in the physical education department; and Whitman was brought in, primarily as the result of a push by Randy Peterson, a member of the board of regents and a former jock himself.

Whitman was a dynamo. In his first year he brought with him a slew of community college transfers and transformed a 1-and-10 team to an 8-and-3 team. By his third year he had transformed the City of Linden into a veritable hotbed of college football. Linden State formed its first "booster group." The sleepy *Linden Times* sports page perked up, greatly increased its coverage of Whitman's program, and gradually started to beat the drum for "Big-Time" collegiate athletics at Linden State.

In Jones's fourth year as president he achieved a childhood ambition: appearing prominently on the sports page. He confirmed that Linden State was moving up to a Division IAA-level program, complete with athletic scholarships raised by the "Vikings Booster Club." Some of the luster of the event faded, however, when, in response to a reporter's question, he confessed he really didn't see Linden State eventually moving up to the Western Athletic Conference despite the fact that an away game had been scheduled with Texas-El Paso in 1997. No, he admitted, there was no truth to the talk about putting Brigham Young on the schedule, but he hastened to add the team would be playing Cal Poly San Luis Obispo, rather than Highlands, next year.

When Whitman's Vikings went 11 and 0 the following year, Peterson and the other boosters led a successful fund-raising effort to refurbish Linden State's decrepit football stadium and to expand the seating capacity from 12,000 to 18,000. The operation also permitted an eventual expansion to the magical 30,000 seating capacity that would be needed when Linden State made the next move to Division IA football.

While the townspeople were ecstatic about the successes of the Vikings, some campus constituents were not. The faculty senate inquired about the process used to determine that Linden State would go "big time," which eventually led to a rather nasty confrontation between the faculty senate president and Regent Peterson at a board meeting. The students were up in arms because they had lost prime seats in the stadium to major donors. Those most malcontent, however, were in Linden State's physical education department.

Hubert Jones, a historian by background, soon learned more about physical education than he had ever cared to know. He even became empathic to the department's concerns, but now that the genie of Linden State's version of big-time athletics was out of the bottle, it was too late to put it back.

The physical education department, like several others, had fallen on hard times as Linden State made its transition from a teachers college to a regional state university. "PE," as the department was called, found itself looked down upon by both the liberal arts departments and the professional programs of the emerging university. As if the department's future were not bleak enough, the bottom had also fallen out of the market for physical education teachers. In response, the department tried to make its curriculum more scientific and demanding and to prepare its majors for more innovative careers, including positions running "wellness" programs for private industry.

Jones himself had indirectly and inadvertently contributed to PE's woes. As a new president he had issued a special challenge to the faculty to revise Linden State's general education program required of all students, to make it more innovative and academically demanding. He was satisfied with the result: the new general education program was indeed more creative and rigorous, especially in its requirement of interdisciplinary "capstone" courses for students at the upper-division level. For PE, however, the new program was another setback: the "personal and social living" category of courses, which included PE activity classes, was cut back from six units to three units.

PE's enrollments went into a tailspin, and the department found itself listed as among the most overstaffed of the university at the very time it urgently needed new blood to complete the revamping of its curriculum. Accordingly, PE saw the movement of Linden State's program to the more competitive Division IAA level as another major threat. Big-time athletics meant still more coaches to be hired and eventually absorbed by PE, no doubt at an even faster rate as coaches burned out under new competitive pressures or suffered losing seasons.

Even if Coach Whitman had not made his next controversial move, PE no doubt would have led the charge to separate the athletics program from the rest of the department and thus relieve the department of the burden of absorbing tenured ex-coaches. Whitman simply brought matters to an earlier head when he first nominated a criminology graduate for an assistant coach position and then refused to accept the department chairman's unequivocal "No!" to the request. The current athletics director, himself a PE instructor, halfheartedly pressed Whitman's case and still the answer was no. Appeal through the school dean and the provost was *pro forma,* and on to President Jones's office came what was by now a hot potato.

Jones remembered the opening salvo well. Whitman made the initial phone call to his office. He mumbled to Jean, Hubert's secretary, about desperately needing to see the president. Jean kept him on hold while she checked with Jones, who told her to arrange the appointment at the earliest convenient time. In a few moments she was back with Whitman's plea for a meeting that very day. Jones decided that Regent Peterson would understand why a previously scheduled meeting between the two of them would need to be canceled, and arrangements with Coach Whitman were hurriedly made. Peterson well understood the urgency of the situation and kept Jones on the phone for a 25-minute tirade against the parochial and jealous faculty members in PE who were making the beloved coach's life practically impossible. Surely, President Jones could handle the situation.

A phone call to the provost prior to the meeting with Coach Whitman brought Hubert Jones up to date on the issues in the dispute. Technically, the provost said, coaches were hired as physical education faculty and eventually gained tenure. In addition to coaching, they were expected to handle PE classes in order to justify their positions: even Whitman was responsible for two or three activity courses in conditioning, although everyone knew that graduate assistants actually covered the classes. In the past PE had always been accommodating in the hiring of coaches but, as Jones knew, the department was under great stress, and this time Whitman's proposal was simply unacceptable. No department could be expected to employ as part of its faculty someone who lacked even the barest of professional qualifications to teach in the department. No one disputed that the young candidate was a most promising quarterback and wide receiver coach. No one disputed that a wide-open passing attack was central to Whitman's strategy for the years to come. Whitman, in turn, would have to admit that a bachelor's degree in criminology was not sufficient background to be employed even at the instructor level by the physical education department. It would be a travesty, the provost told Jones, to have such a person teaching the department's courses, and there simply was no way to employ him without such a teaching assignment. Surely Jones would agree and would help protect the basic integrity of the academic program in this latest assault by the jocks.

Whitman entered Jones's office deferentially but looking as distraught as he did last season when he was down 7 to 0 to Highlands at half time. Jones rose from his chair to greet him and remained standing for the next ten minutes or so as Whitman paced back and forth, mumbling, grumbling, and shouting his tale of woe. He simply wanted the tools to do his job and to bring greater recognition to Linden State, and instead found himself devoting his energies to campus politics, which he disdained. The new assistant coach was central to his plans. Neither he nor any of his staff gave a damn about tenure or the other privileges of faculty status. If the football program were to progress, it needed university support, not an endless series of roadblocks. He had never bothered the president before and hoped he would never have to again, but he had no one else to turn to. Couldn't President Jones solve the problem, he pleaded, in the voice he used in his famous locker room team talks. Let's go out there and beat the hell out of them for good old Linden State!

Jones, who had started the meeting with his customary sense of being in charge, felt like a third-string defensive back being sent in to sacrifice himself on the kickoff special team. He would give it his all, and Coach wouldn't be disappointed.

After Whitman left, Jones called the provost and set in motion a series of events that would lead to the separation of PE and athletics. A new "coaching specialist" position, nontenurable, was created and all the football staff transferred to it. Coaches, housed in the new athletics department, could no longer teach in the physical education department but would concentrate all their attention on their demanding coaching duties. Elaborate arrangements were made between athletics and PE to handle the scheduling of facilities, joint use of the equipment and locker rooms, and so forth. When the two parties couldn't agree on the sharing of costs for towels and cleaning, the dispute came all the way up again to Jones, who successfully pushed it back down again for resolution. When the added costs in instructional positions came up to Jones (four more for athletics, including two additional football coaches and a new full-time athletics director to be recruited from the outside, and two more for physical education), he told the provost to pay the "ransom," faintly hoping he had heard the end of it.

❧   ❧   ❧

Neither Jones nor Coach Whitman had really wanted to play racquetball together. It just happened that their respective opponents had failed to show (in Jones's case, the brash John Carlson), so they played together rather than forgoing the exercise. Whitman started out deferentially and won the first game by a humane 21-12 score. In the second game Jones made two errors: he got off to an early lead and whacked a ball into Whitman's lower back. Whitman's eyes became glassy, and he began to mumble to himself as he served. The second game ended 21-2, and a perfunctory third game ended 21-3, Whitman's favor. Upon leaving the court, the fierce coach mumbled something about opponents who call too many hinders, and only after showering whispered "Nice game" to Jones and scurried to his office to while away the summer hours watching films of last year's Vikings season.

In turn, Jones returned to his office and called John Carlson to ask where he had been. Carlson had forgotten their appointment to play.

Pete Washington had been Linden State's basketball coach for twenty-one years. Twelve of those years had been winning seasons; nine, losing, including five of the last six. His greatest years were the four that John Carlson played. When Carlson called Jones to say he couldn't keep their racquetball date that afternoon, he added that he had lined up "Coach Pete" to stand in for him and that the president would enjoy the game with the venerable Linden State fixture.

Jones did enjoy the game, easily winning the best-of-three match. What he didn't enjoy was learning on the court what Pete Washington was really like. The match, in fact, took more than an hour and half to play, as the coach would take advantage of rest periods and irritating pauses before his serve to lecture the president about the pitfalls and fallacies of big-time athletics. To Hubert the behavior was abominable; he had never found it easy to separate work from home life but certainly had been able to separate it from the racquetball court. Hubert also suspected he saw John Carlson's fine hand behind the captive arrangement in which he found himself.

Chapter Two/11

Coach Pete's thesis was rather simple. Whitman undoubtedly was a great coach, but football had become the tail wagging the dog. You simply couldn't have football at the IAA level and leave the other sports at the nonscholarship Division II level. Moreover, look at Whitman's team: only 12 young men from Linden and its surrounding towns. He, Washington, believed in "playing the kids" and had all locals on his team. The university was doing its local students a terrible disservice by pursuing a self-aggrandizing strategy of moving up to a new level of competition in athletics. And the costs would be enormous. Menacingly, Washington referred to a study done by the physical education department on the escalating costs of athletics since Jones had become president. Even now the department was thinking about sharing the results of the study with the faculty senate's budget committee. Jones should turn the Linden State ship of state back to harbor, chart a new course, and then sail in safer waters. And as captain, sink with the ship, Jones thought to himself while showing off his new backhand kill shot.

Coach Pete had no way of knowing that, as of this summer, Jones had declared himself emancipated of all veiled, and even open, threats. A year earlier Jones would have listened attentively and sought a way to address the concern. But now he simply kept his mind on the game. Later he would come to grips with how he would respond to Washington. When the old coach sat down at game point of the third game and repeated his whole litany, Jones decided his response wouldn't be pleasant.

In the shower, savoring the victory more than disliking the conversation that went with it, Jones found his irritation had largely dissipated.

"Good game, coach. Really enjoyed it. Glad John set us up to play."

"Yeah, thanks, prez," Washington responded. John told me you were getting pretty good. Wish I were a little younger, so I'd be more competition. But don't forget the good advice this old coach has given you. It'll save you and Linden State a lot of trouble."

"Well, coach, things change and grow. Sometimes they go by us. Maybe you're right, but I don't think so. More honestly, I'm not sure it matters. Some things in the university move along on their own momentum regardless of what people like you and me do. Why don't we make the most of our own opportunities while rolling a bit with the punches? Come to think of it, I'll give you a golden opportunity to even up the score from today at your own game."

Washington had difficulty following Jones's reasoning and was suspicious of this "golden opportunity." Nevertheless, he asked the fateful question, "What do you have in mind?"

"Well," Jones went on, "I agree with your premise that sports are for everyone and that there is a virtue in competing with students from your local student body. Why not carry over the same line of reasoning to our Linden State faculty and staff? Tell you what. You assemble a basketball team from among your colleagues in physical education and athletics, too, if you want. I'll make up a team from the other faculty and the staff and we'll have a shoot-out. Bet I can outrecruit and outcoach you."

"Like hell you can," Washington replied immediately.

Jones was pleased the old coach still had some fire left in him.

"Better warn you," Jones added, "I'm going to John Carlson as my assistant."

"You're on, with or without Carlson or anyone else you can dig up," Washington asserted with finality. "We'll play one month after the faculty gets back this fall."

"Oh, there's one other condition," Jones added."Given Title IX implications, each of us has to play at least one woman player at all times. Agreed?"

"Agreed," the old coach responded.

"Okay, then," Jones concluded. "See you this fall and you'd better be ready."

Walking back to his office, Jones was in a glorious mood. He even stopped by the student union, bought an ice cream cone, chatted with several students, and poked his head in to see the union director. The director wasn't in, but that was all right. Jones had really stopped to check on his receptionist, a six-foot redhead who had finished her basketball eligibility and was now working full time while completing her degree.

"Angie, we're having a faculty and staff basketball game this fall. Can I count on you playing on my team?" Jones asked.

"Of course, Dr. Jones," was the pleasant reply. "And I have this friend, Karen, who works down the hall and used to play for the University of Colorado. I bet she'd like to join us."

The first step in his plot accomplished, Jones took the next and went to his office and called the director of the computer center. At the president's request, the director agreed to install in the president's office a more sophisticated computer arrangement than they had originally discussed and to hurry the project along so that it would be completed over the summer. Finally, Jones called Carlson to tell him about the challenge match and his new duties as assistant coach to the president.

3

Change brings pain as well as growth, and so it was when Hubert Jones entered the world of the microcomputer. The primary pain came from having to tear up his pride and joy, his beautiful credenza, to accommodate the new machine within his work space. Secondary pain came from holes drilled through his new paneling to allow wires to be run linking his computer to the campuswide electronic mail system, a feature that Charlie Fisher, the computer center director, insisted he would want despite his mild, and Jean's vehement, objections.

Jones objected to the damage to his new paneling. Jean's objections, Jones suspected, arose from something more profound: she had always sorted his mail, protecting him from trivia and culling out those matters best called to his attention when he was in a good mood. The electronic mail system took away not only her ability to shield him but also a source of her own status at Linden State.

Jean was not the only one leery about the potential impact of the president's new computer. At his next cabinet meeting, Ed Svenson, the provost and a political scientist by background, inquired at length about the extent to which the president's computer would give him access to the data in the computer center's mainframe. When Jones explained that his new hardware worked off "floppy disks" (he hoped he had the right term) and would not be connected directly to the ubiquitous university mainframe, he thought he had answered Svenson's question. Svenson, however, pressed further and within moments was beyond the technical capacity of Jones, the out-of-date historian who had difficulty even making his way through the computerized bibliography recently installed in Linden State's library. Finally, Jones recognized that Svenson's concern wasn't really technical at all: he simply didn't want Jones to have readily available to him enrollment, staffing, and other data that would let him second-guess, and perhaps even abrogate, decisions that Svenson viewed as properly belonging to the provost.

"Ed," Jones blurted out with surprising directness, "don't worry about it. I have no intention of mucking around with the data you all in academic affairs guard so jealously. If I want to know something about your shop, I'll ask you. I assure you that I have plenty to do now and am not anxious to take on more."

Although irritated by Jones's response, Svenson was ready to let the matter drop. Bill Farber, the dean of students, however, was not.

"I find these computers dehumanizing," Farber began. "It seems like those of us in student affairs spend half our time straightening out computer errors that cost students dearly in terms of time and frustration and even delayed graduations. And as for the new financial reporting system, the information is never timely, and we still have to keep all our own books by hand in order to manage our accounts."

Farber's comments led to a counterattack by Bill Bashford, the vice president for business affairs, who was responsible for the computer center. Eventually even Ed Svenson reentered the fray with a remark that the computer center, now that it had the president also hooked, no doubt would be increasing its budget demands for microcomputers by another 100 percent and there would be a further rip-off of Linden State's meager equipment budget for academic programs. Jones reminded his provost that even a 1,000-percent increase in the computer center budget wouldn't meet the demands for computer services. This led Svenson simply to change his focus to the library, where promises in position savings that couldn't be met were made when the new computerized cataloguing system was installed.

At this point Jones simply asserted a prerogative of the presidency, calling the discussion a healthy exchange of views and changing the topic.

Word of the new microcomputer in the president's office traveled quickly, and on a slow news day a local television station came by to feature Jones in a background segment on the impact of the computer on university instruction. Jones waxed eloquently on the impact of new technologies, the need to prepare students for the twenty-first century, and Linden State's leadership position in computerized instruction. He thought the interview was going famously when disaster struck.

"We'd like to have a shot of you at your computer. How about it?" The request of the reporter seemed innocent enough, and Jones rolled his chair around to his credenza for a shot of the with-it president and his personal computer.

"Could we get a shot of you working on something? With the screen lit up?"

Again the request was reasonable, but Hubert Jones felt a knot in his stomach. It suddenly occurred to him that the young man sent over by the computer center to introduce him to his new machine had always turned it on before Jones's lesson. Well, it couldn't be that difficult, Jones surmised, as he searched furtively for the simple on-off switch. None was in sight. Desperately he pressed the keys marked "Esc" and "Ctrl" and went on to the various arrows. Nothing.

"As I indicated to you," Jones remarked apologetically, even sheepishly, "I'm still a novice and have much to learn myself. I'm afraid there's a problem with the machine and I don't have the foggiest notion what it is. Couldn't we simply take a shot focusing on the keyboard instead of the screen?"

Jones sensed from the reporter's disappointed look and response that his suggested alternative simply wouldn't do, so he made an urgent call to his young instructor in the computer center. The bright chap at the other end of the phone eventually translated accurately Jones earnest request, stated in terms that Jones hoped would be disguised from the television crew watching him intently.

"You want to know how to turn the computer on? Is that your question?"

"Yes! That's the problem," Jones responded. "Can you take me through the steps to fix it over the phone? I've got some people here who want to see a demonstration."

"Do you want me to rush right over?" the helpful young man asked. "I can be there in a jiffy."

"No. Let me see if I can handle it over the phone," Jones responded, inwardly squirming. "If I can't, I may need you right away."

Following directions, Jones fumbled about, blindly and by touch, the back of the microcomputer. The close quarters made it impossible for him to see what he was touching. When he thought he had finally located the proper switch, to his horror a wire fell from the computer to the floor under the credenza. After convincing assurances over the phone that he would not be electrocuted, Jones made his way under the credenza, shoved the wire back through a hole, fished it out from the top, and inserted it in the only receptacle he could feel at the back of the computer. In doing so he also accidentially discovered the fateful switch. With trepidation, he went right from his wire act to hit the switch. There was the hoped for ding-a-ding and whirring of the microcomputer and for the moment Jones felt secure again. Now if only he could press on a little further, and if only the television camera had not mischievously caught Linden State's Computer Age president groveling around under his credenza.

Jones thanked the voice at the other end of the phone for his assistance and mentioned, just loudly enough to be heard, a loose connection that might require the computer center's attention, but which Jones thought that he had fixed. He then posed at the computer for the camera and felt silly. With feigned confidence he pushed the keys that would let him enter the first program.

Before he felt taxed, he heard a voice say, "That's great. Hold it right there, if you can." On the screen appeared a brilliant burst of colors, moving in kaleidoscopic effect. The image had nothing to do with the function of the computer and had been placed there for show by the young techno whiz in the computer center, but for television it showed up perfectly and appeared impressive. Or was the reporter unwilling to press her luck further? To Jones it made no difference as he posed with his new, prized posession and sought to appear computer literate.

That night Jones anxiously watched the television news for confirmation that the cameras didn't catch his derriere under the credenza. Deep in his heart, he knew he couldn't have resisted the temptation to run with such footage if he had been a television editor. Fortunately, the story was straight and, Gladys thought, rather impressive.

Gladys, however, was less impressed with Hubert's new fetish during the evenings, as he pored through computer manuals and workbooks. When he let slip that he was thinking about having a computer terminal installed at their residence, she put her foot down. She had other plans for the room Hubert eyed as the future nerve center of Linden State, and Hubert dropped his plan rather than face another awkward conversation about Mother coming to live with them.

Gradually Hubert mastered his personal computer. He also collected on floppy disks a motley assortment of university files, or so it seemed to his young computer center confidant, who was sworn to secrecy about Jones's data and programming needs.

Hubert's crash program met his self-imposed deadline. School would open in three weeks, and the great shoot-out with Washington's team was perhaps a month and a half away. It took Jones a full Saturday morning to run through the various files and programs required to give him just the information he wanted. First he sorted through his abbreviated faculty and staff personnel file, then through the questionnaires that had been filled out by every person expressing an interest in the faculty and staff wellness program. His assistant had coded the data well and had, as instructed, stuck to the essentials Jones had requested. Finally he cross-checked the personnel and wellness files and had the list of faculty and staff he was seeking.

The computer spewed out 27 names. Recognizing the importance of the list, Jones had it printed boldfaced. Here they were: every faculty and staff member, outside physical education and athletics, who saw fit to list his or her previous athletic prowess, who expressed a desire either to get into or to stay in shape, or who was over 6'4" tall. Most of the names were unfamiliar jewels that would have gone undiscovered had it not been for the miracles of the computer age. Carlson and Angie Nelson were on the list. (Jones also suspected that Carlson had exaggerated his height.) Angie's friend, Karen, was not on the list, and no doubt others, too, had been missed. But 27 were enough to choose from, he thought.

John Carlson, in his role as assistant coach, was sent out to scout the 27 prospects. When he came back a week later, he announced that eleven of them were great finds.

"Wow, Hubert, where did you dig up the names?" Carlson asked. "I confidentially felt the eleven out about playing and all but three were game. Funny, Angie Nelson seemed to know already what was going on and said she had a friend who'd play, too. Looks like we'll need both of them, just in case. My main concern, though, is getting Tommy D'Angelo from maintenance to go along. He was a heckuva forward with me in high school ball, but he's ballooned up to 245 pounds."

"Never mind where I got the names," Jones replied. "And leave D'Angelo to me."

D'Angelo was unimpressed by a personal visit from the president of the university, but he did like the time off with pay that went with his new assignment.

After another meeting with Carlson, during which they carefully compared notes on the available talent, Jones had his team.

4

As school was about to open that fall, Provost Svenson was all doom and gloom. The last computer run showed enrollments in early registration to be down 7 percent. Freshman enrollments, always an omen, were down 12 percent, and new upper-division community college transfers were down 4 percent. Even the knowledge that all the provost's news was completely new to the president—showing Jones had not tapped into academic affairs data—failed to cheer Svenson. Even before meeting with Jones, Svenson had admonished the deans to fill classes to their maximum possible sizes, had added many faculty positions in business and speech to gather up last-minute student enrollments in these high-demand areas, and had frozen all operating accounts to underscore the urgency of the situation. An enrollment drop, he explained, would mean a drop in the university's budget for the year.

Each fall, for the past three years, Svenson had similarly panicked and twice had been right to do so. This time his sense of doom and urgency was higher than ever, so he felt anger as well as frustration when Jones seemed calm about the impending disaster.

"Relax, Ed," Jones calmly directed. "You've done what you can. We can't invent students who simply aren't there."

"But have we done everything? And will those bastards in the faculty who are after me—and you, too—believe we have. They're convinced our new general education program is partially at fault; we've made it too tough to get into, and to stay in, Linden State. Students are going elsewhere."

"You know that's nine-tenths bull,' Jones countered. "Anyone following the demographics of our region knows our problem is that we're not hearing right now any echo from the baby boom promising enrollment relief. Enrollments are bound to drop, unless we can draw to Linden State a higher proportion of the potential students who are out there. Maybe our critics are right, Ed. Maybe we were wrong in pushing such a demanding general education program. How about promoting another general education revision? It would give the faculty something to think about other than falling enrollments and disastrous budgets."

"Over my dead body," Svenson shot back. "Every new president sponsors a revision in general education and you've had your turn. Each time we go through the exercise, the academic vultures come out, eyeing every opportunity to increase their own enrollments at the expense of someone else and chewing me up as a by-product."

"Well, we'll see," Jones responded, turning his chair around and flicking on his microcomputer, signaling that the conversation was over.

Except for a postscript two weeks later, the conversation was indeed over. In his opening address that fall to the assembled faculty, Jones began by plugging the faculty and staff wellness program. A few of the faculty were heard to murmur that the president himself was looking surprisingly fit and relaxed given the gloomy forecasts about enrollments they heard from deans upon their return from their summer breaks.

The faculty's mood turned to shock, however, when Jones unabashedly speculated that Linden State's too rigid and traditional general education program might be a cause of the university's present enrollment debacle. Without a hint of apology to anyone, Jones then went on to challenge the faculty to look anew at Linden State's general education program. As he did so, Svenson left the stage, where he was seated with the other notables of the administration, went back to his office, and wrote a blistering letter of resignation, which Jones accepted with a note of feigned regret produced on his microcomputer.

The time for the grudge game with Washington's team was soon at hand, and Jones had to fix his lineup. He wished there had been time for practice sessions allowing him to evaluate the talent on the computer, Carlson, and he had assembled. Also, D'Angelo was grumbling that he might not play because the time off from his routine maintenance duties for such practices had not materialized, but Carlson's renewed friendship with "Tony D," as Carlson called him, enabled him to keep D'Angelo in line.

As Jones saw the lineup, the 6'4" 245-pound D'Angelo would start at power forward and would be the team's inside intimidator. Angie Nelson, at 6 feet, a center in women's basketball, would start at small forward. Kenny Adams, the 6'9" educational opportunity program counselor and the computer's prize find, would start, of course, at center. Kenny had played in the late 1960s at Wichita State and had either kept himself in great shape or had still not learned to eat enough to add pounds on his wiry frame. Carlson would play point guard and would run the team on the court just as Jones saw himself running the team off the court, and Jones would start at the other guard position. Karen Fisher, Angie's friend, two faculty members from education, and a sociologist would be the substitutes.

In reviewing the lineup with his assistant coach, Jones found that Carlson had in mind the same starting five but proposed that Angie Nelson and Jones switch positions. Jones thought Carlson was arguing that he wanted Angie in the backcourt to strengthen the team's ball handling, but Carlson, after some hemming and hawing, insisted Jones had misunderstood. Always quick on his feet, on and off the court, Carlson appealed to the male chauvinist in Jones—it simply wouldn't be right to have Angie butting heads with Washington's oafs under the basket—and convinced the president to make the revision in the lineup.

The game was set for an early Saturday morning in order to accommodate everyone's schedule, much to D'Angelo's distaste, but had to be moved back in time twice because of unanticipated difficulty in selecting an unbiased referee. Washington had suggested that someone from physical education act as a referee, which was unacceptable to Jones. Jones, however, despite the assistance of his computer files, couldn't come up with an acceptable alternative. Finally, Jones and Washington agreed to assign the selection of a referee to Carlson, whom they both trusted, and Carlson leaned on a friend of his who refereed local high school basketball to give up a Saturday morning for a memorable experience.

Washington also sought a delay in the schedule to gain time to recruit the required women players. Then he asked that the affair be changed to an all-men's game. Jones insisted that the original ground rules stand, although he sympathized with Washington on the day of the game when he showed up with a woman PE instructor recovering from a sprained ankle and with the new athletic department's secretary, a good-natured soul who stood 5'2", weighed 152 pounds, and was 52 years old.

It looked as if the game might be delayed again at the last minute when the referee pointed out the obvious to Jones and Washington: it wasn't feasible to play "shirts" against "skins" and he wasn't going to referee if the teams did not wear distinctive outfits. Carlson, though, came to the rescue with T-shirts for Jones's team, green and yellow with the phrase "The President's Body Guards" printed across their backs.

Carlson cautioned Jones that they faced a quite formidable foe. Washington had along with him his two assistant coaches, the women's basketball coach (a man), the golf coach, and a physical education instructor who was formerly on the football staff.

After the customary introductions, handshakes, and selective—given the circumstances—pats on the behind, Kenny Adams easily won the opening tip-off. The ball went to Carlson, who drove the length of the court but came back out and passed to Angie Nelson. Nelson threw wide of Jones, and the ball went out of bounds.

"That wasn't Angie's fault, Carlson chided Hubert as they made their way back down the court to set up their agreed-upon zone defense. "You're supposed to come out for the ball."

Jones didn't have a chance to ask Carlson what he meant. He was too busy coping with Washington, who had him isolated one on one, drove easily around him, and laid the ball in for the first two points of the game.

The next time down the court Adams took a high lob from Carlson and in one fell swoop brought the ball crashing down on the rim of the basket, from which it bounced into the hands of an assistant coach at the free-throw line, who threw it to a huffing and puffing Washington at the other end of the court. Two more points for the opposition, and Washington, who had failed to get back on defense, was looking great.

The score was 12 to 2 when Carlson called a time out. "Don't panic," Carlson intently instructed his team. "Just stick with our game plan. We're a little rusty, that's all. Jones, how about a rest? One of the faculty here can spell you."

The two education faculty members were champing at the bit to play. In fact, as faculty, they had assumed they would be starters. The sociology professor, however, was nowhere to be seen. He had arrived at the gym dressed in plaid Bermuda shorts and Hush Puppies. The Bermudas would do, Carlson had reluctantly conceded, but he would have to find some regulation shoes before he could play.

"No, I'm fine," Jones responded, ignoring the disgusted look from the education professors.

Rather than pressing the point, Carlson noted that Washington's team was actually using set plays. Fortunately, they were the same ones Coach Pete had used when Carlson played for him. He then diagrammed, in Greek, Jones thought, the proper defense and suggested to D'Angelo that he play less tentatively in the middle.

D'Angelo's version of less-tentative play was to wipe out the golf coach on a pick set for Carlson, who whooshed a smooth fifteen footer. Next the intimidator threw an elbow that caught an assistant coach on the side of the head and precipitated an official's time out, during which Washington talked incessantly to the referee. The game had hardly proceeded again when the former football coach went crashing into Tony D., who fell backward into the gimpy female PE instructor. There was another official's time out, to let the PE instructor limp off the court permanently, and this time there was harsh shouting by Washington at both the referee and Jones. When Washington wouldn't settle down, the referee gave him a technical, which Jones put himself forward to shoot and missed.

Jones had cracked under the pressure, standing all alone at the free-throw line. He was also distracted by what he took to be signs of blood on the floor. The next time his team got the ball he unilaterally switched to a three-guard offense by placing himself on the perimeter and ignoring Carlson's blandishments.

By half-time Jones's team was down by only two points, 24-22, and the momentum had definitely swung in their direction. Jones himself had proudly scored four points, and it bothered him not at all that they were at the expense of the 5'2" secretary Coach Pete had disparagingly assigned to guard him. Carlson had 12 points, and only D'Angelo was in foul trouble, with three.

At half-time Carlson disarmed the team's school of education dissenters by producing soft drinks and appropriate snacks, apologizing that he had given all the beer to Coach Washington's team. When it came time for the second half to begin, Carlson started Jones, Adams, the two education faculty, and Karen Nelson. Washington countered with his four male starters and his lone female substitute, who soon petered out entirely and from time to time simply sat down on the court. Playing in effect with only four players, Washington's team was still too much for Jones's revised lineup and widened its lead to 34-28, when Carlson put the "Body Guards" first team, minus Jones, back in. Jones was spelled by the sociology professor, who had returned complete with ancient black high-top shoes his live-in girlfriend had somehow rediscovered for him in a closet. The "soc prof" further disgusted Jones by intimating that he would have been back earlier had he not been delayed by a "quickie."

Jones joined the disgruntled and disaffected education faculty on the bench. Carlson made six quick and unanswered points and the "soc prof" added four more. Washington was hooting and hollering at every referee's call, a sure sign that victory was at hand for Jones's team. By the time Jones got back in—he had to insist that Carlson call a time out to make the point that he, the president, was rested and ready—the score was 62 to 46 with only three minutes to go.

The game ended 68 to 54. Carlson had 26 points, Jones six, and Washington ten. Washington and his team angrily stomped off as soon as the final whistle had blown. That was all right with Jones. After all, as head coach he had congratulatory duties to perform for his victorious warriors.

"Great job everybody," Jones said with sincerity and delight. "We beat them badly and there's no question about who's the best team. Now I'm not going to be long-winded, so let me just say thank you for all your efforts."

Jones also recognized quickly that he would not have the opportunity to be long-winded. His team was drifting off before he had finished his second sentence.

Only Carlson remained behind. "Hey, you were pretty good yourself, prez," Carlson chimed in with pretended sincerity. "But I wonder how Coach Pete is going to take it?"

Jones learned how hard the venerable Coach Peter J. Washington took it when he saw the sports page of the Sunday *Linden Times*. The reporter had learned of Coach Pete's decision to resign through unnamed sources and the coach had confirmed it. Coach Pete magnanimously recognized the need to bring in a new coach who could continue Linden State's progress in basketball. "This has always been a great basketball town," Coach Pete was quoted as saying, "and I hope that my successor will get the tools necessary to compete at the Division IAA level. In particular, we need a new arena, not only to accommodate our growing number of fans, but also to help us recruit top athletes. Unfortunately, the current Linden State administration has not seen fit to give the basketball program that kind of support."

Two hours later Jones's already-ruined Sunday morning was interrupted by a phone call from Bill Johnson, the new athletics director.

"I hate to bother you at home on a Sunday," Johnson began the conversation, "but I needed to apologize to you about the newspaper surprise. I thought Coach Pete would have to step aside sometime soon, but I had no idea he would take himself out so abruptly. I haven't been able to reach him and can't imagine what happened to make him announce his resignation right now. Sure hope he'll reconsider the timing. There's no way we can get a replacement in time for this season, at least a replacement we'd want to have."

"I saw Coach Pete just this Saturday morning," Jones interrupted nonchalantly at his first opportunity. "It was pretty obvious something was bothering him, so I'm not too surprised. I guess I'd recommend we let his decision stand and make do. Have any ideas about who could step in for him?"

"I'm not too impressed by either of his assistants," Johnson replied, "but I suppose we'll have to go with one of them."

"Let me make a more promising suggestion," Jones interceded. "Do you know young John Carlson in student affairs? He's identified with the winningest years we've ever had in basketball. Why not think about him as an interim coach? He'd do a heckuva job, I'm sure. Don't know if we'd have many wins, but I guarantee we'd have great entertainment."

And Carlson would learn a little humility in the process, Jones thought to himself.

"If you think that might be a way to go, I'll gladly give it some thought. I'll talk to him Monday, size him up."

"You do that," Jones concluded the conversation, confident that Carlson would jump at the chance and would charm the daylights out of Bill Johnson.

On Tuesday morning press coverage of Linden State's basketball fortunes looked up. The *Times* reported that Bill Johnson, the athletics director, had made a surprise announcement that Johnny Carlson, the former Linden Lincoln and Linden State great, was taking over as head coach. When Carlson had been reached for comment, he was enthusiastic about Linden State's prospects in the year ahead and announced also that 32-year old, 6'4" Tony D'Angelo was enrolling as a freshman at Linden State and definitely would brighten the Vikings' future.

5

Gladys had outdone herself. The annual president's fall dinner at the university house for the board of regents was certain to be a great success. All was in place. The food was prepared to Gladys's exact specifications by the university food service, the student bartenders—all over 21 years of age—briefed and apparently competent. As Zetas, Jones thought, they should be, but he resisted the temptation to give the student bartenders a middle-aged, somewhat hypocritical lecture on the evils of demon rum, especially under the current circumstances. Even the crack in the living room ceiling cooperated: it was just big enough to be noticed by the regents, to prepare them for the annual presidential complaint about the level of upkeep done by the university, but not so bad as to be distracting.

Unfortunately, the new campus security men charged with parking the regents cars were not so well-prepared. Karl Schultz, the chair of the board, had been sent to the hinterlands to fend for himself. "No, your license number is not on the list. . . . I have my strict instructions, Mr. Schootz. . . . Yes, Mr. Schultz, I meant. . . . Well, I'd check with Dr. Jones, but I wouldn't want to hold up these other cars."

As Karl told the story later that evening, Jones was mortified, but the regents, including Schultz, thought the situation hilarious and went on to invent their own form of 21 Questions, trying to guess Jones's future university assignment.

Most of the evening was delightful. The major exception was a 20-minute conversation in the library between Jones and Regent Peterson. Talk had started innocently enough, with speculation about just how well John Carlson would do as the interim coach.

"Making young Carlson the coach was a gutsy move," Peterson commented. "I understand you were the one who suggested it. He just might surprise everyone. Was Coach Pete's resignation a surprise to you as it was to everyone else? Or did you have some brilliant intuition that let you anticipate that one, too?"

"Well, as I've gotten to know him better, few things Coach Pete does surprise me any longer," Jones responded.

"I agreed with him on one thing, though," Peterson went on. "We're not going far in basketball until we have a new arena. The old gym just won't do anymore. I'd think the students and townspeople would really turn out if we had a new arena. Why don't we see about getting the students to build one? It's their turn. We can't raise the money from the townspeople. I'm afraid we've tapped them dry for some time in enlarging the football stadium."

"I doubt the project would fly with the students," Jones countered. "Besides, they have in mind financing a new auditorium, and many of us believe we need such an effort to counterbalance all the seeming emphasis on athletics."

"Hubert, you're getting as unpredictable as old Coach Pete. Aren't you the very person the faculty is growling about because of all the positions you're siphoning off into athletics? I was rather proud of you. Just what is going on in your head now?"

Jones went into a long, detailed explanation. He knew the community could not be called upon for another major fund-raising drive so soon after the most recent effort. However, the real pressure to expand athletic facilities came from the community, not the students, and so the best tack to take might be to wait until the community was ready to take on a new basketball arena. The time was not propitious to push the students on the matter, since a basketball arena of the size talked about—say, seating 5,000 persons—would cost some $7-8 million. (He had little idea what the most accurate cost estimate would be, but he thought he was in the ballpark—or *arena*.) The student government leaders would totally oppose a fee increase large enough to finance such a huge project. He had even talked to Linden State's legislators about the possibility of state funding assistance but was told that such state participation was absolutely out.

After a mutually agreed-upon "time out" to refresh their drinks, Jones continued his attack and concluded with a ringing declaration of the right of students to set their own priorities for buildings they wished to see funded through fees assessed them by their own vote.

Peterson listened sympathetically for the first few minutes of Jones's monologue, then listened impatiently, and finally listened hardly at all as he prepared his counteroffensive.

"How do the students go about setting their priorities?" Peterson asked with feigned innocence.

Jones explained the students' elaborate committee structure, their careful assessment of options, and the need for a vote of approval by the student body, all of this under the careful and sympathetic guidance of Dean Farber's office of student affairs.

"How many students typically vote in such elections?" Peterson then asked.

"I don't know offhand," Jones responded.

"Well, I suspect not very many," Peterson countered. "Those student body officers you're talking about didn't receive more than 500 votes each out of a student body of 9,500 students. I doubt that a thousand students would vote in such an election. If Farber and you wanted to provide some administrative leadership on the issue, and Carlson got the student athletes to the polls, you guys could pull it off. That's the long and the short of it, isn't it?"

Jones correctly discerned that Peterson's last question was rhetorical and decided to let the matter drop. He was helped in this by the sudden emergence of Audrey Peterson and Gladys.

"There you two are," Audrey declared with some exasperation. "Gladys and I thought we might find you off in some corner, probably discussing athletics again. Come on, there are other things in this world, and you two have to mingle now with the rest of us."

Right on all counts, Jones thought, grateful it had been Audrey and not Gladys who had been so direct.

After dinner Peterson again cornered Jones, but not without a chase through the dining room, living room, library, and kitchen.

"Hubert, when are you going to do something about Dean Farber? From all I hear, he's fallen asleep as the dean of students."

This time Hubert decided to be short-winded.

"I've been looking at our student affairs office," he responded, "and have decided that it has become too insular and that the dean himself needs some kind of new challenge. What I am going to do is this: next week I'm announcing that student affairs will report directly to the provost, not any longer to me, and that Dean Farber will be the acting provost, replacing Ed Svenson."

"I don't remember your discussing such a move with the board, Hubert," Peterson responded, obviously surprised. "Have you discussed it with Karl as our chairman? He didn't say anything to me about it. I assume you discussed it at length with the faculty leadership, as is your inimitable style."

"I didn't discuss the move with anyone. In fact, I only firmed up the decision this evening. Call it administrative leadership."

"Coach Pete called me the other day," Peterson went on. "He said he thought you were crazy. Maybe he's right. I'm pushing the board to a full evaluation of your work as president and I guess we'll find out." Then Peterson went off abruptly for a refill.

As the evening closed, Jones was confident Peterson had not related their conversation to Chairman Schultz, who was in a good mood as Hubert escorted him to his waiting car. It had been driven to the door by a young man who announced he had replaced one of the on-duty officers who had suddenly become ill.

Despite his growing misgivings about athletics, Jones felt privileged when Coach Whitman called to invite him to join the Linden State Vikings on the field at the opening game of the fall football schedule. The day of the game was cold, and Jones dressed warmly—fortunately, because he needed the extra padding as he was spilled to the ground by a lineman bouncing off Linden State's fullback along the sideline. He expected some sympathy but found none. In fact, he heard Coach Whitman, glassy eyed as the Vikings were down by a touchdown, mumble something about damn fool spectators who didn't belong on the field and got in the way of the game.

6

When Acting Provost Farber first related to Jones the outcome of the faculty chair election, Jones's reaction was disbelief. How had Anthony Bacon, whom Jones viewed as a second rater, won? Was the faculty no longer serious in choosing its spokesperson? Farber, however, was pleased with Bacon's election and gave the president an insightful primer on Linden State's faculty politics.

Under Jones's predecessor, Arthur Peabody, the faculty divided tensely on two issues: the increasing importance being attached to research and publication and the possibility of faculty collective bargaining. The campus Old Guard, who supported teaching and opposed both research and collective bargaining, had ruled the campus without challenge for many years. Their technique was careful selection of those faculty who served on key committees and then the cooptation into important faculty leadership positions of those faculty who paid their dues and showed promise and dependability through their committee assignments. These leadership choices were made over lunch in the faculty dining room and then relayed by word of mouth through the Old Guard's informal network.

When President Peabody came down strongly in favor of upgrading Linden State's faculty through an increased emphasis on scholarship, his call for action struck an especially responsive chord in the science faculty, who organized themselves to push for a major university commitment to research. These science faculty members entered into a working alliance with solid majorities in the humanities and the social sciences who favored collective bargaining, and a new grouping called the "Outsiders" soon became a threat to the Old Guard oligarchy. The Outsiders hammered out their choices of candidates in late afternoon caucuses held alternately in the science and the social science buildings, and they communicated their choices through written slates distributed especially to the junior faculty. The latter technique was vastly superior to the grapevine system of the Old Guard, and the Outsiders scored some early spectacular victories in faculty elections.

When the Old Guard finally stopped complaining about the brazen and overt political tactics of their opponents, they proceeded to mimic them. Soon Linden State's tranquil and uninteresting faculty elections became full-blown campaigns mounted by two well-organized political machines. The outcomes were inconclusive and unpredictable, and neither side could win a decisive victory.

To Jones's surprise, the unconventional Tony Bacon had been nominated for the faculty chairmanship by the stodgy Old Guard. As in American politics generally, the party machinery had tended to grow more interested in winning than in loftier issues and concerns. Bacon was seen by the Old Guard as "solid" on the teaching-versus-research issue. On campus governance issues, he was something of a maverick, but at least he was known to oppose collective bargaining in its more adversarial forms. As a maverick and relatively junior member of the social science faculty, he brought to the Old Guard something else it very much needed to win—namely, a good smattering of votes from the social sciences and the humanities to accompany solid Old Guard majorities in education and nursing and smaller majorities in other professional schools.

Jones was surprised by the crisp, knowledgeable manner in which Farber laid out the political machinations leading to Bacon's election. "Has someone been giving you a crash program on becoming a provost?" he asked. "I thought you were a student affairs type. You spun out that scenario as if you had been on the faculty all these years."

"No crash program," Farber responded, obviously pleased by Jones's reaction. "You see, when the Old Guard saw its majority in the faculty was endangered, it sponsored and pushed through an amendment to the faculty senate constitution granting representation to my student affairs counselors. Since that time, student affairs has been courted by both the Old Guard and the Outsiders. I suggested to my people (I hope you don't mind) that they form their own caucus to decide just which candidates to support. Our little bloc has done wonders for our influence and status on the campus. We're forming an alliance with the librarians that should make us even more influential in faculty politics. Frankly, Hubert, your move to combine student affairs and academic affairs into one administrative unit has also given our efforts a real shot in the arm."

During this conversation, Jones caught a glimmer of a Farber he had not seen before. Jones had named him acting provost as a first step toward moving out this over-the-hill dean of students but, surprisingly and disconcertingly, Farber was showing new life in his new role. That afternoon Jones stayed late in the office and wrote five letters nominating Farber, "this distinguished administrator and senior statesman," for administrative openings outside Linden State.

When Dr. Anthony Bacon dropped by for his first visit, Jones still had difficulty visualizing him as the faculty chairman. First, there was the matter of his dress: wash-and-wear brown slacks, an open-collar tan shirt, and a worn corduroy sport coat accented by various pins and buttons signifying social causes. Then, too, in Jones's eyes there was an unpleasant aura surrounding the young man because his doctorate was a "D.U.R.P.," the sound of which Jones associated with indigestion, not scholarship. The thought of the doctorate in urban and regional planning, a professional degree not requiring a standard dissertation, also triggered in Jones the memory that he had delayed Bacon's promotion to associate professor, in part because of the unconventional doctorate but more so because there were no scholarly contributions acompanying what was obviously a superior teaching record.

"It's a pleasure to see you, Professor Bacon," Jones began the conversation, carefully choosing the appellation "professor" rather than the ubiquitous Linden State "doctor."

"And it's a pleasure to see you, Dr. Jones," Bacon replied. "This is the first time I've ever gotten past your very efficient secretary. By the way, please call me Tony. Should I call you Hubie? From the way you blanched, I think not."

"I'd like you, though, to just call me Hubert," Jones replied awkwardly. "No doubt we will get a chance to know one another well this year, and it would be best to dispense with formalities right away."

After a few more minutes of banal conversation, the conversation turned to Jones's appointment of Farber as the acting provost. Unlike Regent Peterson, Chairman Bacon of the faculty senate was not especially concerned about Jones's lack of consultation in making the appointment.

"Your move really took us off balance," Bacon commented. "But the more some of us thought about it, the more we liked it. If you had consulted with me and the rest of the faculty leadership, we never could have agreed to Farber's selection, but I suspect he's just the person for the role in view of what some of us have in mind for Linden State. You see, we've been talking among ourselves about the challenge you laid down to reconsider our general education curriculum. Again you surprised us by calling attention to the rigidity of our program. As a planner by background, I was also pleased you focused on the demography of our region. Dean Farber—oops, I meant Provost Farber—also has some ideas he has discussed with me about making our curriculum more student oriented. Dr. Farber and I will be meeting next Tuesday with the General Education Committee to discuss our views, and we would very much like you to join us to expand on your thoughts. Can we count on you?"

Jones was perplexed about how to respond. He was pleased his views were being sought, but for some reason he also felt irritated. Was it because good old Bill Farber was now "Dr. Farber" and he was "Hubert"? Then, too, he wondered who was included in Bacon's indiscriminate "we." Farber? The Old Guard? Moreover, he didn't have the foggiest notion about what he would add to his earlier comments about general education. They had been made when he was in a cavalier mood, and on later reflection he had decided he liked the program so recently adopted at his own urging.

The mixture of emotions Jones felt eventually sorted itself out: he was flattered his views were sought. "Of course I would be pleased to join you at the General Education Committee meeting," Hubert responded, somewhat ruefully, to Tony.

It was raining on the day of the General Education Committee meeting, and Hubert was self-conscious walking across campus holding prominently above his head Jean's floral-print umbrella. Jean had assured him that the purple and gold coordinated with his suit, but he suspected she was simply trying to put the best face on the situation. As he walked along he was splashed by the wake of a bicyclist who was tearing along the sidewalk oblivious to danger. Why, he wondered, had he not insisted that the committee meet with him in his newly redecorated conference room? The prison-made furniture there was first rate, the chairs plush and comfortable, and the surroundings bright and cheerful—in part, he admitted, because Jean and Gladys had successfully convinced him to wallpaper over the dark conference room paneling.

Once he had entered the social science building, where the committee met, guilt about splurging to renovate his office, including the conference room, came to the fore. The building was drab indeed. Its halls were painted battleship gray, except for one with a once-gaudy mural commemorating the end of the Vietnam War. The mural as approved by the then-extant University Beautification Committee was to pay innocuous homage to spring. Its true outline gradually emerged, and an enormous dispute ensued about the academic freedom of the graduate students who did it. The final result was that the mural stayed, the Campus Beautification Committee disbanded itself, and there were no more murals on the Linden State campus. At present, the peeling mural had little impact on the hordes of students who drifted through the hall, and Jones was surprised to find he, too, was indifferent to its message.

The seminar room in which the committee met was in worse condition than the peeling mural. The table bore the whittled dreams and initials of bored students. The walls were a sickly green, the chairs wooden and uncomfortable. Then there was the pipe and cigarette smoke from three of the six faculty members who were present and from Farber, an inveterate chain smoker.

Jones was late to the meeting and found that the issues concerning general education had already been joined. The academic conservatives, with whom Jones customarily identified, were defending the general outline of the existing program. Phrases such as "standards," "rigor," and "liberal education of the whole person" were strung together in supposedly meaningful utterances. Tony Bacon, in turn, challenged the committee to think in terms of meeting the needs of Linden State's more average students, who attended the university to prepare themselves for the job market and found it difficult to meet in four years, or even five, the current general education requirements as well as the ever-expanding requirements for their majors. Bacon's refrain was echoed by Farber, who argued explicitly that the faculty should fit the curriculum to the perceived needs of students rather than forcing students to master a curriculum based on outmoded notions from an earlier and more elitist era in higher education.

As the argument progressed, Jones found himself lining up votes. It appeared that the conservatives, who favored the status quo, held a slight majority, but the final outcome would depend heavily on a physical education faculty member who had said little as her colleagues rambled. When she did speak, Jones listened carefully, recognizing that her predilections were likely to be of great importance to the committee's deliberations. Her preamble dealt with the previous injustices heaped on her department when compulsory physical education courses had been eliminated from the curriculum twenty years earlier. As to the current program, her department deeply resented rejection of their proposal to include physical education dance courses in the fine arts division of the general education program. Jones figured she would vote for a major review of the entire program. And, he guessed, she would keep her eye on the most fundamental implications of any program that emerged from that review—namely, its implications for her department's enrollments.

"We're deeply divided," Tony Bacon understated the situation. "President Jones has joined us. He highlighted this fall the need for us to review our general education program, especially in view of the enrollment drop we are experiencing. President Jones, perhaps you would like to add something to your previous remarks."

"Well, I think you are doing a good job of getting the issues on the table," Jones began, showing proper deference to the learned faculty. "I'm not sure what I can add. Perhaps it would be best if I responded to any particular concerns or questions you might have."

"I have one," piped up—almost literally as smoke enveloped him—a senior member of the accounting department. "Are you willing to accept the faculty's judgment on the curricular matter before us? My concern is that you and Provost Farber are suddenly becoming very outspoken about general education, and I want to make sure you're only presenting your views for our consideration as the university faculty. Nothing more."

In response, Jones piously reiterated his traditionalist stance that curricular issues were in the faculty's domain. Not surprisingly, he supposed, the discussion was swiftly picked up by the voting members of the committee, who largely repeated their earlier points as each side sought to wear down the other. After listening to enough of the repeated discussion to feign an interest, President Hubert Jones excused himself from the committee's dank quarters, which he now felt they deserved. Once outside the building, he popped open Jean's umbrella, welcoming its bright colors, despite the clearing sky.

7

Thanks to modern technology, Hubert was less tired than usual on the day after the Associated Students fall rock concert. Less tired, but no less irritated.

When he first came to Linden State, Hubert made a momentous, and many thought foolish, decision: he listed his phone number in the directory. Gladys had argued successfully that an unlisted number would make it difficult for their friends and relatives to contact them and had carried the day on the issue. By and large, the Joneses were comfortable with the arrangement, and in truth their evenings were far less interrupted by a ringing phone than had been the case in earlier years when their children were teen-agers living at home. The glaring exception was those evenings when the students had outdoor concerts.

During his first year as president, Jones felt that a true calamity had hit the entire northwest quadrant of Linden on the night of the first such concert. The first outraged calls from campus neighbors came in about 8:30 p.m. from the sick and the infirmed. By nine the odd-scheduled sleepers had joined in. By ten the well and the usually calm were barraging him. By 10:30 the regents and the city council members were calling in response to the many calls from the outraged and the anguished they had received. By 11:00 all of them were calling back, often expressing disillusionment with the new president of Linden State, who had vowed to improve town-gown relationships.

In between their calls, Jones made anxious inquiries to campus security. Fortunately, he had a private line to the security office; the publicly listed number always gave forth a busy signal. In his first conversation with the sergeant-in-charge, Jones had simply requested that the concert speakers be turned down and had naively expected a quick response to his tactful presidential inquiry. In his second conversation he had become more demanding. The third time Jones called—following a polite but pointed conversation with Chairman Schultz of the regents—he ordered that the concert be shut down.

Fortunately for Jones, the sergeant at the other end of the phone was a Linden State veteran and effectively presented the argument for letting the concert run its course. After Jones's first call, a security officer had gone to the concert site and had insisted that the volume be turned down, which the sound man dutifully did. When the Wrackettes—as the performing rock group was appropriately named—threatened to walk off the stage in response, the sound man, at the urging of Assistant Dean of Students Carlson, cranked the speakers back up. After Jones's second call, the sergeant himself confronted first the the timid sound engineer and then the person in charge of the event, namely, Assistant Dean Carlson.

Over the music Carlson shouted his explanation for turning up the sound. The Wrackettes, from their perspective, were not being noisy but merely protecting the quality of their performance. In fact, the amplifiers belonged to the group and had been installed at their specific instructions to ensure that every note, or noise, could be heard by the discerning, if not deafened, ear. Because they felt their artistic freedom was threatened, they absolutely refused to continue the concert with less amplification.

Carlson then pointed to the crowd, the self-evident reason why the concert simply had to continue. Before Carlson and the sergeant bobbed and swayed more than 3,000 of Linden's young people. The rock music had enveloped them, transforming them from a mere crowd into a unified force bonded by bass notes that could be heard for miles. Carlson did not have to convince the sergeant that, unleashed, this force could be destructive indeed. Better to let the concert extinguish itself naturally at 10:30 p.m. as scheduled.

Jones's third call to security came in at 10:52, and the Wrackettes were on their third encore. The conversation lasted some 15 minutes. At first the sergeant was simply stalling in hopes that he could announce to the president that the concert and crisis were over. When the music blared out with the beginnings of a fourth encore, the sergeant placated the president by stating his resolve to shut down the whole affair but insisted on two conditions: he would be absolved of personal responsibility and the president would call the city police and arrange for backup to handle what was bound to be an ugly scene. Jones responded to the sergeant's request with a "see what you can do and I'll call you back later" comment.

Shortly after 11:45 Jones left his phone off the hook: he had had more than enough of playing the accessible president. Unable to sleep, at 12:55 he placed the phone back on its hook and was relieved to find that there were no more calls, at least until 7:30 the next morning when Regent Schultz called to tell him that the matter of rock concerts would be made an emergency item at the next board of regents meeting.

In the interim, the dean of students office hurriedly drew up new guidelines for concerts, including maximum decibel levels for sound amplification, a requirement that only the university's own sound system be used, and a clause to be inserted into all performers' contracts that they would forfeit their fees if they played one note past 10 p.m. Several of the regents sought to ban rock concerts specifically. A student tried to dissuade them from such action by citing the pervasiveness of rock in American music. The regents' legal counsel was more successful in diverting the board from such a tough stance. The regents could not, in his judgment, ban only rock music. To do so would be a violation of the constitutional right to freedom of expression. The possibility of banning all musical events, not just rock concerts, to avoid the legal complications cited by counsel was then considered and predictably dropped, and the regents settled for the new guidelines proposed by the dean of students.

Despite the new guidelines, each year Jones got calls from outraged neighbors whose domestic peace was destroyed by this concert or that. Gladys, in turn, refused to budge from her determination to retain a listed phone. It was just before this latest fall rock concert that the Joneses had worked out a satisfactory solution to their differences. Gladys prevailed in terms of keeping a listed phone; Hubert was accommodated by means of a newly purchased phone answering and recording device.

This particular fall evening Hubert had three times talked to irate campus neighbors complaining about the noise emanating from the campus when he decided to switch on his answering device and to call campus security. A new sergeant was in charge and knew nothing about the sound guidelines approved by the board of regents itself, but of course he would go over and see that the amplifiers were turned down. Jones placed the answering device on the setting that would let him listen as the caller identified himself, just in case a regent called. On the seventh incoming call he quickly discerned Regent Peterson's voice and cut in to take the call personally. Peterson was livid and Jones was activated to recall security, where he was told that efforts to turn down the amplifiers had been met by a threat of boycott by the New Wrackettes. The group had stopped its concert for twenty minutes to argue with the security officer the sergeant had sent over and the crowd had become so unruly that the officer thought it best to let the concert proceed.

This time Jones's third call was to Provost Farber, where he was greeted by Farber's friendly voice on an answering machine. Jones's recorded message was brief and to the point, and within minutes he cut in to his own system to take personally Farber's return call. Farber assured him he would take care of the problem.

On the morning after the concert, as was the case the evening before, Acting Provost Farber again would be called upon to wear his hat as dean of student affairs. He would join Jones for a meeting with the student government officers to discuss the possibility of students financing an auditorium by means of a special fee. Jones assumed Farber would give his full support to the auditorium effort, and he hoped the provost would be at his very best despite the interrupted evening of the night before.

At least Farber was on time for their half-hour strategy get-together prior to their meeting with the student officers. The provost looked only a little tired from the events of the night before and held in one hand his customary morning coffee cup and in the other a lit cigarette, his particular pepper-uppers.

"Sorry to bother you last night," Jones began their conversation. "I know you're carrying a heck of a load this year—as provost and dean of students—and I wouldn't have called you except that I knew if anyone could handle the problem, you could. The one thing above all else we should avoid is another go-around with the regents on the issue of rock concerts. No telling what would come out of it. How did it go?"

"Oh, it went all right," Farber replied. "I couldn't get anything done over the phone, so I went on out to campus. Managed to get to the leader of the rock group during an intermission and got his cooperation. He was complaining that since our sound amplification system wasn't any good to start with, turning it down a bit wouldn't much affect the quality of the performance. When I reminded him of the 10-o'clock deadline, he seemed kind of relieved. The New Wrackettes, it turns out, are now the older Wrackettes, and I think they're losing some of their steam. After the concert, I called Regent Peterson and he seemed satisfied. Hope you didn't mind. Peterson and I have known each other for many years, and I thought I could handle him."

"Mind?" Jones responded. "I'm delighted. Now before we go on to discuss this meeting with the students, let me ask you something. Have you thought anymore about designating someone to act for you as the dean of students? I'm concerned that you're carrying too much of a load around here"

"Well, to be honest," Farber replied, "you kind of took away my options there. I had always hoped to groom John Carlson to be my successor. With him as basketball coach this year, I don't have anyone else I'd care to name to act in my place in student affairs. John's trying to help me as much as he can. As assistant dean of students he's always worked closely with the student body officers. He was once, as you may remember, the student body president himself. He asked if he could help by working with the students on this auditorium issue, and I told him to join us in the meeting this morning. Hope you don't mind."

"I don't mind at all," Jones responded without much reflection. "I recognize you need the help."

Jones and Farber then went over the auditorium issues likely to come up in their meeting. Farber recognized the intensity of the president's commitment to an auditorium when Jones told him about his earlier conversation with Peterson. Jones was determined that Linden State would be the region's cultural center, not simply a sports capital.

Rehearsing the questions the students would raise, Farber pressed Jones about the possibility of state funding, rather than student fee funding, for an auditorium. It was out of the question, Jones was certain. The budget analyst from the state finance office was amazed Jones had even inquired about the possibility. The state had funded the little theater for the drama department, seating some 250 persons, and that was all the state would do.

Jones had investigated foundation grants and had not received much encouragement. A private fund-raising effort was out of the question, too. Arts lovers might contribute funds to supplement a university effort but could not be counted on to carry the major load. True enough, the football boosters had raised $2 million to enlarge and refurbish the football stadium, but even that effort was tough despite the rampant enthusiasm of the townspeople for Coach Whitman's exciting and successful program.

Moreover, the townspeople were irritated that the students had not contributed to the stadium project. Two years ago, when the project was undertaken, the student government officers vocally opposed athletics and tried, while fund raising for the stadium was underway, to cut back the portion of their fees supporting athletics. That effort was beaten back and, in turn, all efforts to get the students to contribute to stadium renovation ceased.

During the debate about the stadium, the student government officers indicated to Jones that they would fully support an effort to build a large auditorium rather than an athletic facility. The student body officers of the following year likewise showed enthusiasm for building an auditorium, but they felt the timing was wrong for it and spent their efforts fighting an emergency $20 increase in tuition imposed by the regents to cope with a severe shortfall in funds resulting from a surprise drop in student enrollment.

Jones felt confident this indeed was the year to push for a student-fee-funded auditorium. His optimism rose in the fall when he met the newly elected student body president, Jeff Barnewall, and discovered his personal enthusiasm for the project. In addition, Barnewall, a senior majoring in marketing, had all the charisma and persuasive skills of a seasoned politician.

Barnewall would be joined this morning by his two vice presidents, one his crony and the other a bearded and scruffy nonconformist who had run on the slate opposing Barnewall. Glancing at his watch, Jones discovered his conversation with Farber had carried them past the starting time for the meeting in his adjoining conference room. He buzzed Jean and learned she had already invited the young men, together with Carlson, to take their places and had offered them coffee, which only Barnewall accepted. Very graciously, she added.

When Jones entered the conference room, he found two snags. First, all three young men were neatly groomed and dressed and he couldn't remember which vice president was from the opposition slate. Second, Barnewall was sitting in his chair at the head of the conference table. To make matters worse, a student vice president sat at the other end of the table, making it impossible for Jones to reverse mentally the head and foot of the table. His first inclination was to ask Barnewall to move; his second, to sit along the side, flanked by Farber and Carlson; and his third inclination, which he followed, was to invite the students to join him for a look at his office.

The quick tour was highlighted by a presidential computer demonstration, first expertly by Jones and then skillfully by Barnewall, who explained he had a similar personal computer in his fraternity room. While Barnewall was seated at the computer, Jones announced their meeting had better start and rushed ahead to reclaim his seat at the head of the conference table. John Carlson, however, had taken over the seat in Jones's absence. With a boyish grin and just a little too much gusto, he deferred to Jones and took a seat next to Farber. Barnewall, in turn, motioned to the side of the table both his vice presidents and sat opposite Jones at the other end.

Jones had envisioned a smooth transition in the meeting from his endorsement of the need for an auditorium to Barnewall's acceptance of the leadership role in the necessary student body deliberations, to the formation of a committee to coordinate the necessary student and administrative tasks ahead. His ringing endorsement went off as he had planned, but Barnewall did not pick up where Jones left off. Instead, one of the student vice presidents began querying Jones. Was President Jones going to respect the students' right to decide their own priorities for spending fee money the students voluntarily assessed against themselves? Wasn't it unusual for the university president to summon the student body officers to his office and then, cutting through all the sham, push them into a project that really ought to be financed by state funds, not student fees? Jones was nonplussed at the questions but at least thought he now knew which vice president was which. Fortunately, Farber and Carlson rescued Hubert and during the next 20 minutes assuaged the first vice president's concerns.

Then came the second vice president's concerns. If the students funded the auditorium, they would want control over its scheduling and programming. The college union board was composed of a majority of administrators and faculty and a minority of students. The administration had vetoed every student effort to have a majority of students on the governing board of the college union, which likewise was built with student fees. What was the administration's intention for the governing board of the auditorium? While Jones struggled to discern which vice president was which, Farber and Carlson again entered the fray. As best Jones could discern, a tentative agreement was reached that there would be no faculty on an auditorium board and the students and the administration would have equal representation. The students were not fully satisfied with this outcome but apparently were willing to accept it if the administration would explore a similar arrangement for the college union. Farber, as acting provost, agreed to discuss the matter with the faculty leadership.

Carlson then brought up the possibility of a truly multipurpose facility. He remembered well his problems as assistant dean of students in controlling outdoor rock concerts. Shouldn't the facility be built to handle such affairs? What about adding conference rooms so that the auditorium could serve as the hub of a conference center? Maybe a system of internal soundproof curtains could make the facility suitable for simultaneous use by a series of smaller audiences? Jones disliked the reference to the auditorium as a "facility" but was pleased that Carlson had piqued the students' interest and had turned the tone of the conversation to a more positive one.

At last, Barnewall, with just the proper sense of timing, took hold of the meeting and brought it to a focus. Speaking with student body president sincerity and Kennedy-style accents on every third or fourth word, Barnewall asserted the willingness of his group to take a leadership role on the issue of a multipurpose facility to serve the needs of Linden State. Students would have many questions about programming, financing, and governance, but it was just possible that with the right leadership and broad student involvement the project could be pulled off. As a first step he would set up a task force to outline a course of action. Would President Jones designate someone from the administration to serve on such a task force?

Jones ruled out appointment of his overworked acting provost and ruefully requested John Carlson to take on the assignment. The students were pleased with Jones's choice—as was Carlson.

8

As Jones coaxed the Plymouth Horizon over another hill, his irritation grew. The mood had started as a general annoyance about having to spend this first warm weekend in early February at a faculty retreat, called by Provost Farber, to discuss once again Linden State's general education program. The annoyance grew when there were no large cars available through the motor pool for the trip and he would have to drive the Horizon issued to him for his own university business. It crescendoed and peaked when Farber began his inevitable chain-smoking in the Horizon's close quarters, and it stayed at that level as he listened to Farber and Tony Bacon, the faculty chairman and third passenger in the car, shout at each other above the engine noise and the whirring wind from Jones's open window.

Jones recognized that Farber and Bacon would lower their voices if he rolled up his window, but that was an action he would take only if Farber would quit puffing away. In turn, his self-image as a tolerant and polite person discouraged his making the obvious request that Farber cease smoking. He had benefited, he guessed, from the university's aerobics class; next, he decided, he would enroll in one of those assertiveness training workshops. In the meantime, when Farber shifted from cigarettes to a small cigar, Jones retaliated by turning on the radio.

Of course, Farber sensed no connection between the lit cigar and the scratchy music from Jones's favorite, but now distant, classical music station. "Good idea, Hubert," Farber commented and then began fiddling with the dial until he caught a country music station that came through loud and clear, turned up the volume, and continued his conversation with Bacon over the resulting din. Spotting a sign indicating that the Tippy-Canoe YMCA retreat center was only 26 miles away, Jones turned off the radio and determined to be lost in his own thoughts the remainder of the way, a defense mechanism he had learned as a boy sitting through long church sermons and had perfected in innumerable adult committee meetings.

Try as he might, though, he couldn't shut out Farber's and Bacon's yakking. Farber was making one last stab at changing the retreat's format in accordance with the recommendation of his counseling staff. It was important, he argued, that more time be set aside for structured recreational activities that would give the faculty a chance to mix and mingle. Likewise there should be more time set aside for small group sessions in which the counselors could act as facilitators. Bacon, to Jones's delight, wouldn't buy Farber's suggestions and stuck to the two concessions he had already made—an afternoon volleyball game and an open bar upon arrival. At that point, Jones decided to captain one of the volleyball teams and set up old Coach Washington as captain of the other. He then quickly and decisively sized up the potential athletic talent that would be present at the retreat. He was actually disappointed when his train of thought was broken by the totem pole signs indicating the entrance to the conference center.

Check-in at the headquarters building went smoothly enough, although Jones was dismayed to find Farber would be his roommate. For spite he stuck Farber with two heavy bags to carry on the trek to their cabin but, feeling remorse, relieved the huffing and puffing provost midway. The cabin was spartan but clean and, to Jones's delight, had nary a sign of an ashtray. His relief was short-lived, however, as he watched Farber improvise by flicking ashes from a hastily lit cigarette into one of two glasses in the room. A moment later he further complicated Jones's life by placing his denture powder beside the second glass.

When Farber and Jones finally made it to the opening "social hour," with its open bar, Jones quickly dumped the provost, scrambled to the bar, grabbed a plastic glass, and stowed it in his jacket pocket.

Jones judged the social hour a success: nary a faculty member took the occasion to lobby him on a heavy topic, and he even enjoyed a spirited discussion about the prospects of Coach Carlson's team continuing its winning ways. Unfortunately, the camp-style dinner was less palatable. The faculty committee charged with providing the booze should also have been charged with bringing an appropriate and fit food supply. In the absence of such forethought, the group ate YMCA-camp style: baked beans, corn on the cob, hot dogs on week-old buns, fruit drinks made from concentrates, and extra strong coffee. As he struggled to keep a lid on the gas growling about his innards, Jones gained a new understanding of a sign in the lodge proudly proclaiming that no boy ever suffered pangs of hunger at Tippy-Canoe. To add to his distress, he suspected his roommate for the night would be flatulent as well as nicotine-puffing.

Dinner over and the retreat's plenary session begun, battle lines among the faculty were quickly drawn. With a few exceptions, the Old Guard sat on the right of the room and the Outsiders on the left. Bacon and Farber sat at the front just a few chairs to the right. Jones purposely arrived late and took a chair at the rear, smack in the middle.

The issues before the group were well worn: they had plagued Linden State many times in its 125-year history. True enough, each reenactment of the drama had a different cast of actors who brought with them new accents and points of emphasis, but the basic plot remained the same. With such a broad outline for the script, Hubert wondered how the last scene in this particular reenactment would end.

As faculty chair, Bacon opened up the plenary session of this august Linden State "faculty retreat" with the usual niceties—including a flattering introduction of Jones—and a statement on the topic for the retreat: a reconsideration of Linden State's general education program. As he proceeded, Jones quickly discerned the direction in which he would have the campus move. Bacon would be true to the "teaching oriented" members of the faculty that elected him, not out of loyalty to that faction but because of educational commitments.

The goal of Linden State, Bacon droned on, should be to fulfill its potential as a regional state university. As such, the university was obligated to serve the people of its region—all its people. He then pointed to charts and graphs, professionally prepared in the Urban and Regional Planning Department, that contrasted the social and ethnic backgrounds of Linden State's students with those of young people in the region. Going from chart to chart, he gradually lost the full attention of the audience, but he closed with a forceful statement that got his point across: Linden State was not being true to its role as the university of the people of its region. Instead it was a bastion of the middle-class and those upper-class students rejected by more prestigious campuses away from home. In particular, Linden State was not serving the minority populations in its region. Among young people in general 11 percent were black, 4 percent Native

American, 3 percent Hispanic, and 6 percent Asian. In contrast, only 11 percent of Linden State's students were minorities, and more than half of these were Asian. The black, Native American, and Hispanic populations were dramatically underserved. Linden State also faced a major challenge in how it would serve the newly arrived immigrants from Southeast Asia.

To Bacon, an underlying cause of this underrepresentation of minority students was the university's elitist general education program, designed to serve the needs of students who had enjoyed solid college preparatory programs in high school. The program forced upon students—in the name of *liberal education*—the old-fashioned, elitist traditions of a faculty from middle-class white backgrounds.

Bacon's prescriptions for Linden State were clear: a return to the earlier, flexible, student-oriented general education program; adoption of an open admissions plan guaranteeing access for any high school graduate regardless of background; a new requirement of ethnic studies for all students; and a return of faculty emphasis on quality teaching and accessibility to students as opposed to an emphasis on publishing mediocre works that would seldom be read and on outside consulting that simply lined the faculty's pockets.

Provost Farber led the applause for Bacon's remarks, which was more subdued than Jones expected because the listeners were not sure he was done. Then Farber was introduced by Bacon as the university's "chief academic officer," to Jones's great irritation.

Farber briefly stated his full support for a more student-oriented general education program. As a former dean of students, he shared anecdotes designed to shame the faculty for its narrow-mindedness. He then restated the purpose the faculty retreat in a muddled manner and began assigning faculty members to what he called "buzz groups." (Apparently, after all, Farber had swayed Bacon to change the retreat's format.) While Jones silently prayed his letters of recommendation would lead to Farber's employment elsewhere, other retreat participants had more proactive responses.

"Provost Farber," chemistry professor Gray interrupted, "certainly you are not proposing that we break up now without an opportunity to discuss the points you and our chair have made? We should spend at least a little time exploring a few fundamental points before we form smaller groups."

"Well, certainly, if you wish, but let's not be too long at it. We've outlined a process for this retreat that has been very successful at our student affairs conferences, and we should try to stick with it," Farber responded.

Gray began the predictable counterattack to the views of Bacon and Farber. Linden State presumed to be a "university," or at least called itself one. As a university, it must promote research by the faculty. It must uphold quality and standards. It was ridiculous for faculty members to try to teach science to students who, despite the present admissions requirements, needed remedial work in mathematics and science. Admission standards should be toughened up, not loosened. The general education program, as it stood, barely encompassed enough rigorous science courses. He would not be party to watering it down further.

Faculty members reinforced Gray's counterattack by asserting that students coming to Linden State were also remedial in their writing skills; that students were majoring in applied fields such as business, nursing, and engineering and desperately needed the breadth and rigor of Linden State's current general education program if they were to be truly educated; and that it was a great disservice to send Linden State students out into the world with a degree that was debased.

Farber especially was placed on the defensive when pressed about how many of the minority students had been admitted through special action by the admissions office? How many of those were athletes? What proportion of minority students, other than Asians, were graduated? What proportion of the athletes graduated (more specifically, of the football players)?

The discussion rambled on quite predictably for nearly two hours. Jones listened and dozed alternately. As a historian he used to find categories like "liberal" and "conservative" helpful aids to sort out positions taken in such arguments, so for a while he attempted to place speakers in such camps. When that got too complicated, he searched for new categories and decided that "pro-access" and "pro-quality" might do. Finally, he settled on ugly-sounding categories from his newly found computer world and divided the faculty into three groups: those concerned with "inputs," or access and admissions standards, those concerned with "outputs," or quality and graduation standards, and those concerned with "throughputs" or just whose courses would be required in whatever curricular choices were made. After all the "input" and "output" elements had been put on the table, Jones was confident that those most concerned with "throughputs" of benefit to their particular departments would emerge as a major force that would move discussion from ideology and educational philosophy to concrete decisions.

Chapter Eight/49

Finally and mercifully, Chair Bacon brought the discussion to a halt. His stock went up with Jones when he also announced the cancellation of Farber's proposed buzz groups. Instead, the morning would be spent in recreation, the highlight of which would be a volleyball game for those who signed up. President Jones himself would captain one team and "Coach" Pete Washington the other. Bacon's stock also shot up with all of the faculty when he announced that the bar would reopen in 15 minutes.

Jones had struggled over the last hour to stay awake, let alone appear interested, so he decided to turn in. He was just sleeping soundly when Farber burst through the cabin door, tipped over a chair, fumbled about in the dark, turned on the glaring, shadeless light hanging from the ceiling, and then shuffled to the bathroom. For the next ten minutes the serenity of Tippy-Canoe was broken with the sound of running water, grunts and groans, and flatulent staccato bursts. When Farber finally emerged from the bathroom, he inquired three times if Jones were sleeping. Feigning sleep, Jones decided a fourth inquiry from Farber would be his last and began preparing his defense for involuntary manslaughter—or, as Bacon would call it, "personslaughter." Fortunately for both of them, Farber finally decided to turn in, but not before closing the cabin's windows. As Farber snored away, Jones wondered if people pass gas in their sleep and debated whether he should get up to reopen the windows. It seemed that he had no sooner fallen into a light sleep when he was awakened by a cheerful and fully dressed Farber declaring that last call for breakfast was in ten minutes.

Jones skipped the Tippy-Canoe breakfast—pancakes, cream of wheat, toast, watery orange juice, powdered milk, and syrupy coffee—in favor of an extra hour's sleep needed to handle his grudge volleyball game.

To most participants the volleyball game was a disaster, but to Jones, all in all, it was a joy. Of course, the game did get off to a slow start: there were eleven serves before the referee, a physical education professor, reckoned there had been a legal return. Once that referee had been booed off and replaced by Bacon, the game proceeded in accordance with the anything-goes rules appropriate to its middle-aged participants. Along the way, casualties mounted. There were three sets of sprained fingers, two sprained ankles, and a flattened Mary Smith from anthropology, who had gotten in the way of aggressive Charlie Gray from chemistry. Gray was effusively sorry and Smith was grudgingly forgiving, although she also made it clear

Gray had lost her vote. Another near casualty was Provost Farber, who received on top of his head a hard smash from Jones. This time Jones was effusively but insincerely sorry, while Farber laughed it off and enjoyed the attention.

Washington's team won the first game, 15 to 8, and Jones's team the second, 17 to 15. The score of the third and final game was tied at twelve when Jones went back to serve and spotted Farber, flanked by a quaking Mary Smith, in the opposition's back row. Jones's remorse about his treatment of Farber dissipated as he seized this opportunity to lob three serves in the direction of Farber and Smith. The first fell at the feet of cringing Mary Smith. Farber awkwardly hit the second out of bounds. The third also squirted out of bounds off the outstretched hands of Pete Washington, who had huffed and puffed from way across court, pushed Farber aside, and lunged wildly but too late at Jones's gentle floater.

Victory was indeed sweet for Jones, and he ate heartily at the Tippy-Canoe lunch featuring reheated hot dogs on buns that were now one week and a day old. Jones's good mood even lasted through the first hour of the continued debate on general education that followed. Washington, in turn, had chosen an uncharacteristic seat among the Outsiders and sulked through the discussion.

By the second hour of the debate, every point had been made several times and Jones's euphoria gave way to a dull stupor eventually—and forcefully—interrupted by the sight of Coach Pete Washington rising to speak. Washington launched into a confused but effective tirade against the abuse and misuse of student athletes at Linden State. Young men who lacked adequate high school preparation for success in college were being admitted to Linden State solely because of their athletic skills. Then, after they had given much to the university, they were tossed aside and left to fend for themselves. After four years they had nothing to show for their university experience but a few newspaper clippings and battered and bruised bodies. Washington had resigned from coaching rather than participate in this sham and shame of Linden State. And, his voice rising, he demanded to know where the president of the university stood on this and the other issues the faculty had been struggling with the past two days. The president, after all, was ultimately responsible for the well-being of the university and it was time he spoke.

"Chairman Bacon," Hubert Jones called out as he stood to address the snarly faculty glaring at him, "I agree fully it is time for me to speak."

"Up to now I have listened carefully," Jones lied, "as you all struggled with the momentous educational policy issues at hand. Provost Farber has done a fine job presenting concerns we in academic administration feel strongly about, and I thought I should wait until I was called upon to enter the fray lest you think the administration of Linden State was seeking to usurp the proper and dominant role of the faculty on the matters before you. It's uncomfortable for you all to be turning your heads to look at me back here while I speak, so with your permission I would like to come up front."

As Jones made his way to the front, his competitive instincts stirred, and he resolved not to lose this newest challenge tossed out by old Coach Pete. His mental computer whirred quickly and seized on a strategy that just might work. By the time he had taken his place, smack dab in the middle of the first row, and had turned toward the audience, he had a mental outline. From such outlines in the past he had developed whole 50-minute lectures, and he knew that, once started, he could ramble enough to be able to organize his thoughts further along the way.

Jones started with Gray's familiar theme that Linden State was indeed now a university. He then acknowledged Bacon's concern about Linden State's continued responsiveness to all the people in its service area and connected Bacon's theme to the call for reform sounded so eloquently by Coach Washington. It was time, Jones went on, for Linden State to take advantage of the flexibility inherent in the concept of a university as opposed to a college. It was time for Linden State to begin acting like such a university, not a glorified teachers college that was a university in name only. Each of the various arguments raised at the retreat was legitimate; each vision presented could improve Linden State University. The problem was that the faculty approached the problem envisioning the old Linden State College, not the new Linden State University, and demanded that only one argument, one vision, be accepted.

Warming to his subject, Jones called for a fresh perspective, one based on the Linden State of the future. Linden State University should become—in fact, not just in title—a true university. It should view itself as a collection of colleges, each with a general education program and admission standards appropriate to its particular curriculum and student clientele.

Looking around the room, Jones sensed he had wooed Gray and the Outsiders, but not Bacon and the Old Guard. Fixing on

Bacon, he went on to call for a new two-year "General College" within the university that would adopt an open-admissions policy. The faculty of this college should include the finest teachers at Linden State. Upon completion of its two-year course of study, its students should be fully prepared to enter into the other colleges of the university at the upper-division level. The details of such a plan would need to be worked out, of course, but Jones was confident his vision for the university was practical. Turning to Washington, Jones asserted that he wanted a Linden State that would ensure that the young athletes to whom Washington referred would find their educational needs forthrightly and effectively met—not just athletes, of course, but all young persons who came to Linden State in hopes of bettering themselves and receiving that precious result of their labors: a quality degree from a quality university.

The trip back from Tippy-Canoe sped by for Jones as he and Bacon talked about implementation of the resolution, passed with only one dissent—Washington's. Thanks to Jones, Bacon asserted, Linden State University would never be the same. For Farber, however, it was a long trip: Jones had nixed his smoking.

9

Now that the second semester was well underway, Jones was having second thoughts about ending his presidency. When the school year started, he had intended to enjoy himself, get some things done he had always wanted to do, and then step out gracefully. Well, on the whole he had been enjoying himself, at least more so than during the last several years. In particular, he no longer felt so pressed. He was working 45 to 50 hours a week and staying home many weeknights. Seldom did he put in those 70-to-80-hour, four-and-five-work-nights-out-in-a-row weeks that in past years had become standard practice. Additionally, his new schedule, including an aerobics class each morning at 7:30, followed by a warm and relaxing shower, was doing wonders for him.

But the things he really wanted to get done weren't going quite right. Carlson was thriving, not learning humility, as the interim basketball coach. In fact, even Gladys insisted that they go as often as possible to watch Coach Carlson's exciting team. Then, so far, there had been no job offer to Farber. In fact, Farber seemed to be enjoying his role as the acting provost a little too much, and his name was being tossed about as a possible permanent appointment to the post. In addition, Jones saw no progress by the students on the auditorium issue. He so much wanted that auditorium: it would be his legacy to the campus. From time to time he rationalized he should stay on as president a while longer to ensure that his beloved auditorium would be built, but then he always realized the die had been cast. He had simply mucked up too many things this year ever to receive a favorable evaluation from the regents' subcommittee, chaired by Peterson, that at this very time was reviewing his stewardship as president. If the die had been cast last September, the dice had been thrown and had come up craps that fateful fall evening when Peterson and he had visited in the library of the university house. If he had known Peterson was going to chair his evaluation committee, maybe he would have approached their conversation differently. Or maybe Peterson became chair of the committee *because* of their conversation.

Although Jones had a malicious streak for Carlson and Farber and didn't regret the added pressures they were facing as a result of his actions, he genuinely regretted the impact of his new administrative style on his loyal and competent secretary. Given his new schedule, it fell to Jean to explain to this or that caller that the president simply wouldn't be available this year to meet with them or attend their functions. She handled the task with considerable tact and skill and kept to herself any concern she might have that she was developing a reputation as a barrier to the normally accessible president. Her job was further complicated by Jones's new proclivity to see students with problems, in earlier years the special province of Farber before he became acting provost and then too busy to see such students himself.

Jones had established the office of the provost in his fifth year at Linden State, when, he now recognized, he was already beginning to disengage himself from the demands of the presidency. All key administrators formally reported to the president through the provost, who acted as a superordinate vice president. In presenting the new arrangement to the board of regents, Jones emphasized he wanted time freed to devote to external relations and fund raising. The truth was, Jones's interests were primarily academic and internal to the university, not external, but he had come to realize that Linden State had tried—sometimes adopting and sometimes ignoring—every major academic notion Jones had for the institution. He hoped that a powerful and creative provost would bring fresh challenges to the university. Svenson, the former vice president for academic affairs, had accepted the post with high hopes and great expectations and had believed Jones when told he would have a free hand. When Jones found himself constitutionally unable to stop meddling and dabbling in academic matters, Svenson understandably resigned. Being honest with himself, Jones had to admit that Farber was an attractive choice as interim provost because he expected Farber to defer to him as the president on academic matters.

If a desire to move in and out of academic issues without resistance from an effective provost had motivated Jones's appointment of Farber, that, too, was another matter that didn't work out as intended. As the year progressed, Hubert took less and less interest in academic as well as external affairs. However, the demands on Farber as provost, and the resulting vacuum in student affairs, created a new outlet for what Hubert perceived as his considerable talent as an administrative generalist. He took to dabbling in student problems. At first he saw a trickle of students who couldn't get time slots in Farber's busy schedule. As the year progressed, that trickle became a flood.

Jean usually arranged for President Jones to meet with students at 9 a.m., shortly after he returned to the office from aerobics class. At that hour he was fresh and eager to launch into whatever adventure his student encounters would bring him. Jean had been skeptical that President Jones would stick with his exercise program and was pleasantly surprised both that he did and that it had such a positive effect on him.

Aside from an occasional bike ride with Gladys, the aerobics class was the only aspect of his summer exercise kick Hubert stuck with. He gave up racquetball on the day Coach Whitman stung him three times in the kidneys with hard smashes off the back wall. His bicycling routine had been interrupted by the onset of winter. Remembering how self-conscious he was when he first joined the aerobics group, Jones himself was surprised he had not dropped out.

As luck would have it, his motivation to stay in the program was reinforced by the faculty member, Elaine Loosey, assigned as his exercise partner. The two of them hit it off in the very beginning, in part because they were physically evenly matched, although Hubert suspected his younger and trimmer partner held back in the early days in order not to embarrass the president of the university.

Hubert thought Elaine was about 35, although her figure suggested a younger age. At first he wasn't aware of her physique, nor she of his, carefully disguised in a baggy sweatsuit. On the day Hubert—ten pounds lighter—came to class in his fancy new sweats, Elaine greeted him in tight leotards with a skimpy and bulging top. From time to time, Hubert sensed Professor Loosey was a bit flirtatious but then dismissed the thought as absurd or as the wishful thinking of a man over 50. The relationship didn't blossom beyond the aerobics class, although Hubert did give one guest lecture in Elaine's "Human Development" class. His topic was the role of exercise in ancient Greece, and he thought he had given a sterling performance. The students appeared not to understand the relevance of the lecture to the class. Nonetheless they followed suit with Professor Loosey in giving him an enthusiastic round of applause when the bell marking the end of the class period sounded while he was in mid-sentence and three paragraphs from his conclusion.

Fresh from his second shower of the morning, Jones would rush across the campus from the gymnasium to his office to tackle the problems of the day. His burst of energy and enthusiasm would last about an hour or two as he spent this time helping students. His first act of presidential clemency—some would call it interference—was on behalf of a weeping international student whose parents were caught up in a revolution in her country and thus had been unable to forward her sufficient funds to pay Linden State's tuition. Jones simply waived the tuition, ignoring the warnings of the admissions office and his chief fiscal officer. These warnings focused on the dire consequences when state auditors discovered that the strict legal requirements concerning nonresident tuition had been violated. Jones didn't plan to be there when the auditors showed up, and the rapid passing of the tears, replaced by a gorgeous smile, were his reward for an act of kindness and good will. The international students office praised the president for his compassion and proceeded to send in his direction five other students with similar problems. This praise, however, turned to harsh criticism when Jones, who approved the waivers for the first two students, sent the others back with instructions that the the international students office should handle its own problems.

Jones's interventions for the financial benefit of other students involved fewer complications but were nonetheless deeply appreciated by those who enjoyed the president's personal attention. There was the call to the campus security office canceling the string of parking tickets gathered by the young lady who limped painfully into his office and claimed she didn't understand the need for a special permit to park in the spaces reserved for the handicapped. The student made Jones feel he was indeed a miracle worker as she bounced energetically out of his office. Then there was the waiver of nearly a hundred dollars in library fines enabling a poor young man to be graduated at the end of the first semester. In between there were small loans to students, with no set repayment schedule. Then, too, Jones reached into his discretionary funds to enable six extra cheerleaders to accompany the football team to its big game against Sacramento State University and to enable a brass quintet to enter a regional competition in Denver. The bill for the first trip was a little high because the president provided extra support for a three-day side trip to San Francisco, but Hubert was repaid more than adequately when the cheerleaders led a "Hubert Jones" spell-out at the last home football game.

At the beginning of the school year, Hubert carefully avoided interfering with the academic processes of the university, but as the year wore on he became bolder and more assertive even in this regard. Students had the right to appeal the grades given by instructors to a faculty committee, but to win a student had to demonstrate that the instructor had been "arbitrary and capricious." The faculty committee heard the case and rendered its judgment in the form of a recommendation to the president, who was fully expected to accept as final the committee's judgment. Although it was widely thought that the committee in the most egregious cases sought to negotiate a change in grade with an instructor, no one could remember a time when an instructor's judgment had been formally overturned by the committee and certainly not by the president, who was expected to be the firm supporter of the professional autonomy and academic freedom of his faculty. The committee had struggled mightily with a case involving a student who had been hospitalized during the time of a midterm examination. The instructor had a policy of no make-up examinations and refused to budge when first members of the petitions committee and then the dean of his school pushed him to change the student's grade. Three semesters later the petitions committee issued its learned and convoluted recommendation, criticizing but ultimately upholding the judgment of the instructor.

Horror and shock tittered through the faculty dining room when the word spread that the president had arbitrarily changed the student's grade from an "F" to a "C." Jones had first considered requiring the instructor to administer a make-up examination but decided ultimately to deal with the matter more conclusively. He trusted the faculty member to grade such an examination fairly, although grudgingly, but he pitied the student who would have to bone up on materials now two years old. Also Jones was confident that the faculty as a whole would come to his side once they became aware of the details through the grapevine. Even if they did not, he thought, he had the satisfaction of being right.

The second time Jones interfered with the academic processes of the university he was less certain he was right, but he couldn't resist helping the forlorn student who had come to him as her last resort. A single parent of five children, she was three grade points short of the requirement for admission into the graduate program in social work. The dean of social work was willing to admit her but the graduate school dean, who viewed himself as the protector of Linden State's standards, had unequivocably turned down her admission. Jones hated confrontations with graduate school deans, so he tactfully instructed Provost Farber to handle the problem. Farber as dean of students had clashed several times with the graduate dean and relished in this case asserting his new academic prerogatives as provost. He went confidently from Jones's office to the graduate school to carry out the wishes of the president. Two weeks later he returned to Jones's office to get a written order to the graduate dean, questioned the wisdom of the order, and then sent an assistant provost to carry the mail to the graduate dean.

As the second semester wore on, Jones saw fewer and fewer students at his own volition. His reputation as a soft touch had spread too far, and the flow of students into his office was more than even he cared to handle. He also came to recognize, somewhat too late, that his actions followed the old law of physics that for every action there is a equal and positive reaction. He still enjoyed his exercise class with Elaine Loosey, but he had less verve in the hours following it. Instead of hurrying to his office following the class, he now walked slowly and frequently dreaded the meetings that would follow.

Two of those meetings were with student affairs directors from the admissions, financial aid, and international students offices. They were anxious to reach some better understanding of just how the president wanted them to handle the thirty or more requests from international students for tuition waivers. Ultimately Jones sent them off with brusque instructions to solve their own problem and a tacit pledge on his part to refrain from future interventions. His irritation with the financial aid director grew when he showed up again within a week, along with the athletics director. The two of them were especially grim and quizzed Jones at great length about the circumstances surrounding a loan of fifty dollars he had made to a student who turned out to be a member of the ski team. Fortunately the student had repaid Jones promptly (one of the few such students to do so). Nevertheless, Linden State was in hot water because of the president's action. The extent of the damage was a written reprimand to the university from Linden State's athletics conference and three evenings of homework for Jones as he pored through tomes of rules and regulations from the conference and the National Collegiate Athletics Association. It was the trauma of this event that led Jones to ask Jean to divert the forlorn from his office.

Then, too, there were interminable meetings with Tony Bacon, the chair of the academic senate, together with the members of the academic petitions committee. The senate was considering a new charge for the petitions committee and wanted the president's input because of his obvious interest and personal involvement in the work of the committee. The reason for his involvement in drawing up the revised procedures finally became clear to Jones when the faculty representatives presented their provision that the judgment of the petitions committee would be final and not subject to administrative review. Jones would have gladly conceded the point to them if they had made it during their first meeting together. Out of pique that the group had caused him to waste several mornings getting to the real point of their discussion, Jones purposely dragged the discussion out and ultimately agreed to confused wording that would permit the president to remand a case back to the committee for further review and left the rest ambiguous. Convinced they had made their point, Bacon and his colleagues accepted the compromise wording and left. Jones then called Bacon and agreed to wording that explicitly left the final decision on a grading dispute in the hands of the committee. Bacon assured him that his gesture wasn't necessary, and Jones assured Bacon that as president he'd prefer to stay out of grading matters.

Perhaps the most awkward morning meeting Jones had was with Provost Farber and the graduate dean. When Farber had requested such a meeting, Jones had insisted it wasn't necessary. However, the graduate dean kept the pressure up, and eventually Jones agreed. Farber was uncomfortable throughout the discussion. By this time Jones had become expert at retreating from his activist role on behalf of students and nodded along as the dean went through his litany. When it came out that the older student who had been forced onto the graduate school was doing "A" work, Jones also recognized that the meeting wouldn't be too painful.

On a late February morning Jones felt spring in the air as he made his way across campus from the gymnasium to his office. His mood was good, especially since he had won his bet with Elaine Loosey over who could do the most sit-ups. Victory was worth the dull ache he felt in the small of his back, which had been stretched beyond its middle-aged limits.

As Jones entered his office complex, he was somewhat surprised to see an obviously troubled young man seated in the waiting area. For the past several weeks Jean had expeditiously directed such students to other offices. What was special about this one? He thought he recognized the student. Wasn't he in Elaine Loosey's class, the one in which he guest lectured? The student acknowledged the president with a "Hello, Dr. Jones," which Hubert did not return as he went directly into his office, where Jean quickly joined him.

"There's a student here you should see, Dr. Jones," Jean asserted calmly but forcefully. He has a problem I don't think anyone else can help him with."

"Oh, Jean," Jones replied, "come on now, you can find someone else to send him to. I'm just starting to repair my reputation with the faculty and the student affairs people, and I don't want to start playing ombudsman again."

"Dr. Jones, please believe me," Jean responded. "You should be the one to see this particular student."

"Well, all right," Jones muttered. "Just, though, what is his problem?"

Jean didn't respond; she was already out the door and ushering the student into the president's office.

Jones couldn't draw an early fix on Ernest Johnson, the anxious and tense student who sat across from him. He was a handsome lad, probably over six feet in height, and well dressed. He was indeed a member of Professor Loosey's class, and as near as Jones could figure out he had decided to see the president on the very day Jones had guest lectured.

Finally Jones sought to move away from the small talk they had together up to this point. "Ernest, something obviously bothers you considerably. Would you like to tell me about it?" Hubert asked. "Maybe I can be of some help."

"How well do you know Professor Loosey?" Enest asked in return. "I mean, are you and she good friends?"

"I really don't know Professor Loosey very well," Jones responded. "Does what you are here to see me about concern her? If so, I assure you I shall be as unbiased about the matter as can be."

"Well, Professor Loosey says that only you know about her research project," Ernest continued. "I figured that you wouldn't know about it unless the two of you were pretty close, though maybe you would know about it because you're the president of the university."

"Ernest, why don't you just tell me what's on your mind," President Jones asserted calmly but forcefully.

Jones wasn't prepared for what followed. This was Ernest Johnson's second class with Professor Loosey. When she had asked for volunteers to assist her with her research, he had not stepped forward, but then she insisted that he had special qualities for a very special research project she was undertaking. The project was a sensitive one, and Professor Loosey put him through a long interview before he was fully and finally selected to assist her. He also had to agree never to mention the project to anyone, under any circumstances.

Ernest didn't fully understand where the research project was going, but he trusted Professor Loosey, at least until their session after yesterday's class. It was then that she told him their next session would be at her house that evening and would involve some things that might strike him at first as kinky. He should bring his bathing suit for a time together in the hot tub and should expect a late night. It might be best if he told his roommate he would be spending the night out. Somehow the whole thing didn't sound right to Ernest Johnson, and he wanted some assurance about Professor Loosey from President Jones before going on with the rest of the experiment.

Jones, of course, found the young man's story simply incredible. There must be some misunderstanding, but in any case Ernest should tell Professor Loosey he could no longer continue as a subject in such an experiment. Just when Jones was about to suggest to Ernest he seek counseling, Jean buzzed him and indicated he was already late for his next appointment. Following the interruption, Jones sent young Ernest Johnson on his way with an invitation, which he hoped would never be accepted, to keep him informed if he ran into difficulty in dropping out of the experiment.

Jones was ill at ease the next morning as he exercised beside Elaine Loosey. She, in turn, seemed perfectly relaxed, which confirmed in Hubert's mind that Ernest Johnson was a troubled young man who could do great harm to an innocent faculty member like Elaine. Hubert debated telling her about his encounter with Ernest but decided not to. No matter how the conversation might go, their relationship would never be the same. However, he decided, that might not be too important. Sometime during that morning Hubert decided he would drop out of the aerobics class.

As the next few weeks slipped by, Jones was relieved that Ernest Johnson did not come back to see him. Nor did he ask anyone to follow up on his tale of faculty unprofessionalism. With each week that passed he became more and more convinced he was right in not mentioning the incident to Elaine, and he even found himself considering rejoining the aerobics class. No doubt he would be assigned a different partner and that, too, might be for the best.

The extra early morning hour in the office allowed him to whittle down the mound of paperwork that accumulated during the school year, and Jean showed no sign of resentment about coming in at 7:30 herself to guide Jones as he selected work to handle himself and work to delegate. Jones also balanced his earlier starting time with an earlier departure from campus and, now that the days were getting longer, had resumed bicycle riding in the late afternoon.

As he was preparing to depart at 4:00 one afternoon, Jean told him that there was another student he simply must see. This time it was a young woman. Thank goodness it was not Johnson, Hubert thought.

Edith Schmidt was uncomfortable talking to Jones with the door to Jean's office open a bit, but Hubert was not about to change the routine Jean and he had worked out for the times he saw women students. Finally Edith opened up. With anger in her voice, she got right to the point. She was making a charge of sexual harrassment against a faculty member. Hubert was prepared to assure her she could speak frankly with him and to ask if she would like Jean, his administrative assistant, to join them, but Edith Schmidt needed no such assurance. She spewed her venom quickly and efficiently: Professor Elaine Loosey had propositioned her boyfriend. She wanted something done about it.

This time there were no inquiries about President Jones's relationship to Elaine Loosey. Nor did Edith Schmidt show any signs indicating it was she, and not Loosey, who had a problem. When she stomped out of the office, she had the president's assurance that something indeed would be done. Jean came in right after her departure and asked if there was something she could do to help. Indeed there was, Hubert responded. She could get Provost Farber on the phone immediately. The provost had a problem that needed his prompt attention.

The name of the provost's problem was Elaine, and Hubert had a hunch that Elaine was a problem old Farber could solve.

10

Gladys and Hubert barely made it to their seats before the tip-off marking the beginning of the nineteenth game for the 14 and 4 Linden State Turkeys (nee Vikings). Hubert blamed Gladys for being late and she blamed him. Their bickering began as soon as Gladys sensed they would not arrive in time for the introductions of the starting line-ups and the forming of the "human tunnel." She had read in the *Linden Times* that her favorite player and the Turkeys' leading rebounder, Tony D'Angelo, might not start because of a shoulder injury. There was speculation that "Tony D" might have a shoulder separation as the result of crashing to the floor in the Turkeys' 67-43 romp over the School of Mines. He wasn't needed for the remainder of that game, but he would be sorely needed tonight, in more ways than one, as the Turkeys faced rugged South Dakota State. Every night when Hubert arrived home from the university, Gladys quizzed him about Tony's status, and every night he admitted ignorance. On this day of the big game he had made it a point to drop by the athletics director's office and casually inquire about D'Angelo's status. When he got home, however, Gladys did not make her usual inquiry. She already knew from her hairdresser that Tony D's injury was less serious than originally thought, and he was listed as a probable starter.

Hubert marveled at the enthusiasm shown by Gladys and the other fans as they formed a "human tunnel" that completely encircled the basketball court. Clapping their hands in unison as the players made their grand entrance and circled the court within the tunnel, the fans truly became participants in a "town-and-gown" happening. He understood Gladys's irritation this evening when it became clear that her spot in the tunnel, just behind the Linden State bench, would either be empty or filled by another. But wasn't their tardiness at least partially her fault? After all, she had been late getting home from the department store where she had gone as soon as she learned from her hairdresser that a new batch of bright green

Turkey sweaters, complete with logo, had arrived. It wasn't his fault she had had to wait in line for 20 minutes. Moreover, he really didn't feel a need to wear what had become the official Linden State game outfit, and he was doubly irritated both because Gladys had bought him the extra-large size and because, once again, he required it.

Had they not been delayed, Hubert rationalized, they would not have had the parking problem for which Gladys blamed him. Within moments of arriving it was clear to Hubert that the parking lot near the gym was full, so he confidently went to a nearby faculty lot where evening parking was reserved. Again no luck. At last he offered to let Gladys out while he meandered over to his private space next to his office. It would be something of a walk to the gym, but the air was fresh and cool and the walk would be good for him. Gladys, growing more irritated, muttered that she would accompany him.

As typically happened in the evening—and too often during the day—his private spot was taken, as were all the others in the lot. Exasperated, Jones made his way back to the gym, where he spotted an open space on the lawn in front of the building between two other parked cars. Confidently pulling his Horizon over the curb, he maneuvered into a cramped space between a small Cadillac and a Mazda RX70. As he opened his door to get out, he heard footsteps and shouts coming in his direction.

"Hey, mister, you can't park here. Can't you see this is a lawn!" The voice belonged to a stockily built young man Jones thought he recognized from last year's football team.

"Well, certainly some people are parking here, lawn or not," Jones responded.

"Those cars are driven by the A.D. and Coach Carlson," the young man responded authoritatively. "You'll just have to go elsewhere. Absolutely no one else can park here, not even media. Are you with the press? If you are, we have some reserved spaces for you behind the gym."

"Young man, do you know who I am?" Jones asked in a rising voice.

"No, mister, and I have my orders directly from the A.D. himself," came the reply. "Now, come on, get moving."

"But I am the president of the university," Jones went on, trying to control his voice in a presumably presidential manner. "And this property is part of the university, and I have the right to park here."

The young man started to explain to Jones that the gym was part of athletics' property, not the university's, but thought better of it, turned his heels, and went off mumbling to himself. Gladys, in turn, made a snide comment about Hubert's lack of clout on campus, which only darkened his mood.

When Jones earlier in the year had advocated fund raising with a more academic emphasis, as opposed to a massive effort on behalf of a new basketball arena, he had enjoyed the enthusiastic support of the faculty and students of Linden State as well as Gladys's admiration. Regent Peterson and various townspeople grumbled a bit but appeared to accept the decision. As the year played out, though, Jones gradually came to realize his decision to push John Carlson as the interim coach was not working out the way he had intended. More and more, it looked as though it might be he, not Carlson, who would learn that lesson in humility.

The faculty remained somewhat immune to the basketball fever that gradually infected Gladys, the students, and the townspeople. Only too late did Jones realize Carlson's true genius in mobilizing such support. He should have been aware of it as early as the first game.

Not to be outdone by Coach Whitman and the football program, who once had arranged for Jones to lead the marching band into the stadium to the strains of "Stars and Stripes Forever," Carlson innocently asked Jones if he would be willing to sing the National Anthem at the opening basketball game. In a frivolous mood, Jones actually accepted. Later, of course, he panicked and called Carlson back to say it was out of the question.

To Jones's horror, he found he had called too late. Posters announcing the president's musical debut at Linden State had already been distributed and radio spot announcements were already on the air. Carlson, though, assured Jones he had an idea that would solve everything.

Jones's rendition of the National Anthem, in fact, was a hit, thanks to Carlson, who came up with the gimmick of a narrated version, with the prize-winning University Madrigal Singers providing background support. When Jones midway through forgot the words, he again had Carlson to thank. There they were, flashing in bright green across the fancy new scoreboard. Fortunately, Jones had earlier dropped his objections to the beer ads that adorned the scoreboard, which had been donated by a local brewery at Carlson's behest.

Jones's smash debut was confirmed later that week at his barber shop, where he received friendly reviews and ribbings.

There were only some 300 fans at that opening game. By the fifth home game, when Jones again attended because Gladys had been asked to be an honorary coach, there were more than a thousand fans. Gladys's experience as an honorary coach marked her conversion from the disinterested president's wife perfunctorily attending another university event to a raving member of Carlson's "Green Force," as the fans were becoming known. For the occasion she had purchased a new green sweater and yellow skirt, and she looked positively cute to Hubert, who decided maybe he didn't know her quite as well as he thought. Like other converts he had studied as a historian, Gladys became a "true believer" in Coach Carlson and the contributions of basketball to players, university, and community alike. Hubert could see the depths of her convictions in her wardrobe with its green sweaters, dresses, suits, blouses, belts, and shoes. When she bought a green nightgown, he realized things were out of control.

By the seventh home game, when the Turkeys were 11 and 2 for the season and the 2,500-seat gym packed, basketball seemed on the mind of everyone in town. At church an usher discreetly congratulated Hubert on how well things were going at the university because of the basketball program, and the sermon that very Sunday was based on some analogy between Carlson's team and David's plight in facing Goliath, a comparison that eluded Jones but earned the minister a week of plaudits.

By then Jones found his barbershop conversations were always about basketball. At first the comments were all positive, and Jones basked in the sunlight emanating from Carlson's Turkey Five as the team became known. Gradually, though, Jones found himself ominously in the shadows. When was the campus going to build that new arena so desperately needed? Did old Coach Washington really quit because of a lack of support for the program by the administration? Could Jones get eight extra tickets for the big game?

Finally, but reluctantly, Jones decided to leave the barbershop, which had been one of his favorite haunts. Gladys had been urging him for several years to go to her beauty shop, and she was delighted when he announced his willingness to make the change. No more scalpings, she thought, and to mark the transition, she bought him a man's hair dryer and made an appointment for him with her favorite "hairdresser," tactfully avoiding the term *beautician*.

Hubert's first trip to the beauty shop was on a Saturday morning, the only time he could get free, and was nearly disastrous. The waiting area was crowded with women he hoped he did not know, or at least did not know him, as he gingerly made his way to the appointments desk. "Yes, Dr. Jones, we have you down for 9:30," the young women said too loudly, "but we're running late, so please just have a seat." Jones stood in a corner until a seat became available. Out of place amid all the women obviously enjoying the morning out, just as he had enjoyed his sojourns to his favorite barber shop, Jones decided to thumb through a magazine in order to look busy. His efforts to find one that held any male interest failed, however, and the best he could come up with was a well-worn copy of *Readers Digest* featuring an article on fad diets.

Finally his name was called (too loudly again), and he sidled off to a rather private part of the shop where he was greeted by Augie, Gladys's hairdresser. Augie soon put him at ease with a fishing story, assured him he would appear to have much more hair by having it cut short on the top, and suggested to him forcefully that he come in on a weekday, not Saturday mornings. Somewhere along the line, however, the conversation shifted to basketball. Augie made a special point of crediting Mrs. Jones for his new-found interest in Linden State's Turkey Five.

The full import of Gladys's transformation hit Hubert as he watched the middle-aged woman seated next to him (dressed in green sweater and yellow skirt adorned by three "Go Turkeys" buttons) jump up and down and scream at the referees and opposing coach. "You're blind as a bat!" "Sit down, Coach!" "Steps! Steps! He walked. Wake up out there!" "Boo! Booo! Booooooo!" And then in an aside, eyes glaring at him, "Hubert, as president of the university, can't you do something about this lousy refereeing?" Hubert didn't respond to Gladys, whose attention and mood quickly shifted as all 240 pounds of Tony D'Angelo slam-dunked off a fast break, sending the crowd into euphoria and nearly tearing the rim off the backboard.

And what a crowd it was! Nearly 3,000 fans jammed the Linden State East Gymnasium (renamed from the "men's gym"), designed to hold no more than 2,500 spectators. Folding chairs filled every nook and cranny where bleachers did not extend, including a row of chairs right along the basketball court itself. Where spaces were too cramped even for folding chairs, people stood.

At half time the Turkeys were down by four to South Dakota State, but the crowd was at least momentarily more interested in the half-time extravaganza promised by the coach on his new morning radio show than in the game. The lights dimmed, the marching band struck up "Turkey in the Straw," and Hubert watched as several alumni, whom he recognized as the principal mischief makers at last year's commencement, made their way onto the floor and began hooking up exotic wires and equipment. Green-and-yellow spotlights began shooting about the gymnasium and the basketball pep band proceeded to belt out the Linden State "fight song." Eventually the green-and-yellow lights focused on a spot on the balcony opposite Jones, as did the eyes of every member of the crowd. There it was—the new Linden State mascot—a presumably human form dressed as a turkey. The humanoid raised his wings high and bared a green chest with "Linden State" spelled out in bright yellow letters. As the crowd gasped, the turkey took off from the balcony, wings thrashing away and, after what seemed to Jones an eternity in the air, came to a safe landing close to the intent group of engineering alumni, who quickly swooped up the wires and equipment that had made the "turkey's" flight possible.

As the mascot, joined by the cheerleaders, entertained the crowd with a new dance, proudly called the "turkey trot" by the public address system, Gladys shouted above the noise into Hubert's ears, "Wonderful, Hubert. Just wonderful!" She didn't seem to hear his reply, "And damn dangerous, too," and he didn't tell her his plans to meet with the athletics director and the head of the cheerleaders on Monday morning.

Of course, it had been Carlson who had led the recent drive to change Linden State's team's nickname from "Vikings" to "Turkeys." It had started with his tongue-in-cheek allegation that the Viking mascot was insulting to his Scandinavian heritage, an assertion echoed by Regent Peterson. Next there was the establishment of a student-faculty committee to review the school mascot issue. Coach Whitman and the football program preferred the ferocious image of the Viking. Carlson and his supporters went for a Vampire mascot. The Turkey was an eventual compromise, but Jones suspected it was Carlson's preference all along.

In the second half, Gladys and the other spectator-participants were delirious. Linden State quickly turned the tide and went from 4 down to 6 up, a lead that was never relinquished. The Turkey choreographed the crowd's "human wave" routine round and round the gym. The cheerleaders rose to the occasion, and the old gym seemed to rumble and shake with the din of the crowd's favorite cheer. "The Force—is—with you! The Force—is—with you!"

With two minutes to go, Carlson called a time out to put in his reserves, who had been carefully drilled on how to run out the clock and shoot free throws. Actually, Carlson didn't like to call these players "reserves" or "substitutes" and instead referred to them as his "specialty team," a gesture that had impressed Gladys in her stint as honorary coach.

During the time out, Hubert caught a glimpse of an intense altercation between a well-dressed man at the gymnasium entrance and Regent Peterson. Excusing himself from Gladys, Jones squeezed out of the stands and made his way to the entrance.

Peterson was obviously beside himself with anger, and the other man was equally perturbed.

"Jones, I'm glad you're here," Peterson exclaimed. "This man claims to be the fire marshal and insists we close down the game forthwith. It seems he had a complaint this evening from a supposed fan about overcrowding. The damn fan, he admitted, sounded drunk and was more concerned about having to wait such a long time to use the restroom than he was about fire safety regulations. Nevertheless, he insists we have to stop the game. If we then can thin out the crowd to the 2,500-maximum allowed by the fire regulations, the game can restart. I told him as a member of the Linden State Board of Regents I would see that nothing of the kind happens. Now that you're here, Jones, you handle it. I've got to get back to the game."

As Peterson left, the game restarted. The crowd was shouting and stomping so much that Jones had little idea what specifically the fire marshal was ordering him to do. As the game ended, Jones thanked the fire marshal for his patience and cooperation, carefully folded the citation he was given and placed it in his pocket, and then left himself to rejoin Gladys, who had not missed him.

The meeting with the athletics director on Monday morning would have to wait until after Jones had had his opportunity to confer with the campus legal counsel. When Jones got home after the game, he unfolded the citation and read its mysterious wording. He wasn't sure, but he thought this time he was in real trouble as he read the section on fines up to $10,000 for willful refusal to follow the instructions of a duly authorized fire marshal. Then, too, there was the other little note the marshal had scribbled and handed to him along with the citation: "You wouldn't have these problems if you'd get on the stick and build the new arena the Turkey Five both deserve and need."

11

As the year had progressed, Jones had gained a new respect for the contribution Farber had made as dean of student affairs. He wrote letters of recommendation for Farber less often and even stopped scanning the *Chronicle of Higher Education* for possible openings that would suit the acting provost. True enough, he would not want his successor to be stuck with Farber as a permanent provost, but he did feel a president could do worse than retain Farber as dean of students.

Who would make the best kind of provost for Linden State? Jones didn't know: it depended so much on the personality and interests of the president, whoever that would be. Because he had planned to step out at the end of the school year, Jones had purposefully delayed the selection process for the new provost. At first the faculty had been very concerned about the delay, but then word spread that Farber was being given a chance to see how he could handle the position for a longer-than-usual time as acting provost. Jones was somewhat surprised that the faculty had not seen in his delay tactic his overall strategy to step out himself, but it also painfully dawned on him they might know but just not care.

Gladys, who knew Hubert best, sensed that as the year went on he had doubts about his resolve to leave the presidency, but he explained to her it was already too late to change his mind. If he didn't resign, the regents, led by Peterson, were likely to take him out. Thoughtfully, in view of the uncertainty, Gladys also dropped her quest to have her mother come live with them.

The predicament in which he had gotten himself depressed Jones. So often a president is dismissed after a long period of faculty unrest, but, on the whole, Hubert found his faculty agreeable colleagues. Sure there were pains in the behind, arrogant souls, and prima donnas, but Jones had been prepared for that before entering administration. After all, he had come to his position by way of faculty leadership posts, and Gladys had reminded him more than once of his own foibles when he was a brash young faculty politician.

Just what, Hubert wondered, had he accomplished as president? For what would he be remembered? He had survived in the post for eight years. Wasn't that enough? No, he wanted to be remembered for more than that. Perhaps he would be known as the president who reorganized Linden State as a true university with relatively autonomous colleges controlling their own curricula. Or, more specifically, for the new open admission General College he would propose at the next meeting of the board of regents. The thought of the reorganization that had resulted from his call to reexamine Linden State's general education program made Hubert shudder. He didn't want to be remembered as the father of the General College. The truth was that he had worked hard to establish the very arrangement he was now undoing. So often he had wondered at the peculiar outcomes that resulted from the manner in which universities tackled issues. He saw the General College as another example of the unpredictable results of such efforts, and he liked neither this particular result nor his own part in causing it.

What he really wanted to be remembered for was the campus auditorium he had supported despite many objections. He even dreamed that one day the university would see fit to name that auditorium after him. But his beloved auditorium just might not get underway during his presidency. Feeling he had lost track of the students' progress on the issue, Jones decided to ask Barnewall, the student government president, to brief him on the results of the students' consideration. Perhaps some timely presidential intervention would make the difference between a successful launching of the project and further delay into a future year.

"Hello, there, Mr. President," Barnewall began their conversation in a friendly voice.

"And it's good to see you, too, Mr. President," Jones replied. "I appreciate your coming by. I've heard very little about the auditorium project, and I wondered if you could bring me up to date."

"Be glad to," Barnewall went on. "I should have been in to see you much earlier, but I had midterms to get through and a little argument to settle with the student senate about the powers of the Associated Students president. Must sound familiar to you. The senate is as afraid of my having too much power as my vice presidents were about your motives in pushing us to support an auditorium. But be of good cheer. I have great news for you. I am confident the building project will be supported and funded by students. We have all our ducks in a row and will run a student referendum on the project some ten days from now. I brought along the materials we'll be distributing to inform students about it. I'm sure you'll be impressed."

Barnewall handed President Jones a glossy brochure with a picture of what looked to be a basketball arena on its cover.

"We've consulted with everyone on campus we thought would have an interest in the project," Barnewall proceeded cheerfully as if he had not noticed Jones's sudden look of dejection and despair. "The music, art, and drama departments as well as the college union programming people. Coach Carlson also gave us some insights into the needs of the athletics program. He was great to work with. What we have here is a true multipurpose facility that will meet a variety of needs on the campus. Turn the page there. You'll see how the facility can be used for various events. It'll seat nearly 6,000 people for a lecture or a concert and 4,500 for a sporting event. The way the Turkeys are playing, I hope that'll be enough."

Barnewall looked to Jones for a reaction. There was none from the dumbfounded president.

"The nice thing about the basketball usage," Barnewall went on, "is that Coach Carlson tells us we probably can get community people to pay for half the project. We're going to sell them seat options. Right square in the center of the court. Otherwise all the best seats would go to students, since we'd be the ones paying for it. We're also proposing that students not start paying in to the fund for the project until the community seat options are sold, and we'll use the community-generated gifts as our required up-front moneys. That way, today's students, who are voting on the project but will be out of school before it's built, won't have to shell out dollars for something they may never get to enjoy. That's a nice wrinkle Carlson suggested, and it sure should help us get a favorable vote."

"It's an interesting project," Jones responded in a flat voice. "But I guess I expected to see something that looked more like a typical auditorium."

"You sound a bit like the professors in music and drama," Barnewall responded. "They have all kinds of concerns about the acoustics and are skeptical about the use of curtains to divide the facility into smaller theaters, but in the end they came around. After all, this is a student project and I had to tell them that a multipurpose facility of this kind is the only way students will go for it."

Barnewall's political acumen was sharp, and the students subsequently voted by a two-to-one margin to approve what became known informally as the "Barnewall-Carlson Arena."

🙶   🙶   🙶

As Jones prepared to meet with the chair and vice chair of the board of regents, Karl Schultz and Randy Peterson, to go over the agenda of the last board meeting of the school year, he debated about immediately offering his resignation to them rather than first trudging through the two major agenda items—namely, board consideration of the multipurpose arena and of university reorganization. In fact, he fully intended to do just that as he climbed the steps to Karl Schultz's second-floor office. His resolve was still with him as he opened the office door.

Schultz and Peterson were alone, seated at Schultz's usually cluttered desk. The desk had been cleared. On it were only three glasses and a champagne bottle.

"Hubert, you're a little late, but that's all right," Schultz commented, winking mischievously at Peterson.

"Maybe we should hold up our news for him, too," Peterson added. "Let's not, though. Hubert, sit down and pour yourself a glass of champagne. Better yet, sit down and let me pour."

After glasses had been filled for all three men, Peterson proposed a toast to "Hubert Jones, President of Linden State for, we trust, many years to come." Nonplussed, Jones joined in the toast.

"Hubert," Karl Schultz explained, "Randy here shared with me yesterday the report of the evaluation committee he chaired. The committee was especially impressed by the way you dealt with the basketball arena issue. Carlson pointed out to us how well you handled the students. And you have real supporters among your faculty, especially that fellow Bacon, and among your fellow administrators. You're especially lucky to have had around you a loyal fellow like old Farber. Too bad he's leaving us."

"Randy and I called a special executive session of the board this afternoon, prior to our getting together here, and I'm happy to say that the board was unanimous in voting continued confidence in one Hubert Jones. With your leadership, who knows what's possible for Linden State!"

"That's the way we all feel about you, Hubert," Peterson added. "Don't take me wrong; I am not simply a 'jock regent,' but I like especially the way we're set up to move along in athletics. It's more than the new arena. It's young John Carlson as our new basketball coach. Who else would have thought to put him into the breach, and his success is your success. And as Coach Whitman pointed out to me, that General College of yours is the salvation of the football program. He now has a place to put the young men with potential, but with academic problems, that he needs to move us to the next level of competition. You and I, Hubert, don't always think alike, but I look at the bottom line and, in your case, that bottom line looks mighty good."

For Jones the graduation ceremony that May was indeed a *commencement,* not the farewell he had planned. As he reviewed the accomplishments of Linden State's students in the past year, the loudest cheer rang out for Coach Carlson's conference championship basketball team, and the second-loudest cheer went up when Jones announced Carlson had agreed to stay on as coach. Tony Bacon, as the new dean of the General College, read with great dignity the citation for Provost Farber, who had indeed decided to retire from Linden State but to remain in higher education. He had accepted a new position as assistant to the president at Fresno State University. When Hubert shook his hand warmly and offered his personal congratulations, Farber with equal warmth urged him to come to Fresno for a visit. He added that Elaine Loosey would be going with him, and they would both be delighted to see their old friend.

About the Author

Like his fictional counterpart, Harold H. Haak has had ample opportunity to observe the inner workings of the university. He has been president of California State University, Fresno since February 1980, after serving for six years as chancellor of the University of Colorado at Denver. He also held administrative posts as vice president for academic affairs and as a dean. Prior to entering university administration, he served as an officer of two faculty organizations and as an elected member of the Statewide Academic Senate of the California State University system. Dr. Haak received his B.A. and M.A. from the University of Wisconsin and his Ph.D. in political science from Princeton University.

3 6877 00219 9403